LEARN TO
crochet

LEARN TO
crochet

EDITED BY **Sally Harding**

PHOTOGRAPHS BY
John Heseltine

Coats
Crafts UK

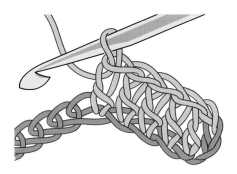

Copyright ©2005 Coats Crafts UK

First published in Great Britain 2005 by
Coats Crafts UK
Lingfield Point
McMullen Road
Darlington
Co. Durham DL1 1YJ
UK

14th reprint -June 2013

Editor Sally Harding
Design Anne Wilson
Illustrations Kate Simunek
Photography John Heseltine
Styling Susan Berry

All rights reserved. No part of this book may
be reproduced, stored in a retrieval system
or transmitted in any form or by any means,
electronic, recording or otherwise, without
the prior permission in writing from the
publisher.

**British Library Cataloguing in Publication
Data**
A catalogue record for this book is available
from the British Library

ISBN 1 904485 32 4

Reproduced and printed in Singapore

Contents

Introduction

Crochet can be used for a wide variety of fabric textures, ranging from a dense, hard-wearing one to a delicate lacy one, depending on the hook size and yarn weight chosen. It is surprisingly quick to create, particularly when using larger hooks and thicker yarns. It has many uses, including acting as an excellent finishing device for knitting garments: joining seams, for example, or creating a neat edging to a sleeve or neck opening. A few sample edgings are shown on pages 26–27, but there are many different ones to choose from.

Although out of fashion for some years, crochet is now very much back in popularity, and is being used increasingly by today's up-and-coming textile designers. Its return has heralded a range of interesting household soft furnishings, such as cushion covers and throws, as well as great variety of accessories, such as hats, bags and scarves. Crochet is ideally suited to these items, as it is quick to work and there are some great, but simple, textural stitches.

This book explains the basics of crochet in a comprehensive, clearly illustrated step-by-step section. Crochet is simple to learn, but the dexterity needed to manipulate the hook and yarn does take a little practice, so try making some small stitch samples in the principal stitches, double, half treble and treble crochet, to make sure you can work easily and evenly. After that you can pick out designs form the gallery of projects, from the very simplest, such as a scarf, to more complex patterns, such as the lacy cushion, which require more skill. As guidance for which projects to tackle if you are a beginner, each project is marked with asterisks to indicate complexity: one asterisk indicates a simple project, two an intermediate project and three an advanced project. Beginners would be advised to start with the easiest and work their way through to the more advanced ones.

Many of the projects in this book are worked as straight pieces of crochet, but if you wish to work 'in the round', which involves increasing the stitches in the 'rounds' to make circular items, follow the instructions in the relevant patterns (see also, page 22).

Equally, you can create an interesting mesh fabric, known as filet crochet. It is relatively easy and quick to work, and is great for producing figurative images as, like cross stitch, it is based on a system of squares making it is easy to design your own geometric filet crochet motifs.

A simple scallop pattern is easy to work and makes a great texture for a cushion cover (see pages 54–55). A similar pattern can be used to create attractive edgings (see pages 26–27).

Yarns and threads

There is a wide range of crochet yarns available. Special crochet cottons are the easiest to work with, but you could also use string, wire, or even leather, if you wish. Coats make a number of excellent crochet threads. Two of the most widely used are *Coats Mercer Crochet* and *Coats Aida*: mercerized cottons that wash beautifully and never lose their colour or elasticity. They come in a number of different thicknesses, from the finest (No. 100) to the thickest (No. 5), all in pure cotton.

Generally, the finest crochet threads are used for lace-like crochet, such as the filet cushion on pages 68–69, the lacy cushion on page 62–65 and the Christmas decorations on pages 72–77.

For a thicker, more solid crochet fabric, you can use 4ply or double-knitting (DK) cotton or wool yarns. These are ideal for crocheted afghans (see pages 58–61) and for cushion covers (see pages 34–41).

To calculate how much yarn to buy if you are using a substitue yarn, use the yarn information on page 79.

Here are the different types and weights of yarns used in this book. At the top are wool yarns in 4ply and double-knitting weights. Below left, centre and right are the special crochet yarns in typical weights and textures, and bottom right are skeins of pearl cotton embroidery thread, which comes in a vast range of colours and is suitable for small projects (see coin purse on pages 52–53).

Hook types and sizes

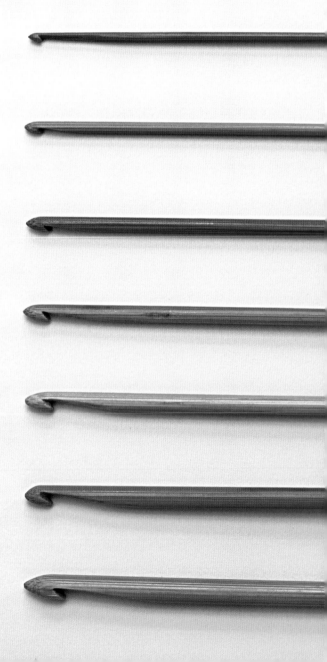

There is a wide range of crochet hook sizes to choose from, and the hooks are made in different materials. Formerly only steel or plastic hooks were available, but there is now a range of bamboo hooks, right, which are great to work with – they feel good in the hand and the yarn slides on and off smoothly. They look more attractive, too!

The choice of hook size is determined both by the yarn used in the project you are working on and the degree of laciness of the stitch. The table opposite gives all the hook sizes and shows how the different hook-sizing systems compare.

The larger the hook and the thicker the yarn, the quicker your work will grow.

A selection of bamboo crochet hooks in popularly used sizes. The finest are generally used for lace-like crochet, the thicker ones for working with thicker cotton and wool crochet and knitting yarns.

Crochet hooks sizes

The crochet hook sizes quoted in the instructions in this book are metric sizes (with US sizes in parentheses). Different countries have different hook-sizing systems (and, to make things more confusing, some countries have more than one system). The conversion chart below shows how the various hook sizings relate to each other, though in many cases the conversions do not match exactly. Metric sizing indicates the diameter of the hook.

HOOK CONVERSION CHART

EU Metric	old UK	US sizes
.60mm		14 steel
.75mm		12 steel
1.00mm		11 steel
1.25mm		7 steel
1.50mm		6 steel
1.75mm		5 steel
2.00mm	14	
		B-1 (2.25mm)
2.50mm	12	
		C-2 (2.75mm)
3.00mm	10	
		D-3 (3.25mm)
3.50mm	9	E-4
		F-5 (3.75mm)
4.00mm	8	G-6
4.50mm	7	7
5.00mm	6	H-8
5.50mm	5	I-9
6.00mm	4	J-10
6.50mm	3	K-10½
7.00mm	2	
8.00mm		L-11
9.00mm		M
10.00mm		N-13
12.00mm		0/P-15
15.00mm		Q
20.00mm		S

Other materials and equipment

You can add buttons, beads, cords, fringes and tassels to finish off crochet projects.

It helps to give a professional look to projects if you add smart finishing touches. Scarves look good with fringes, either beaded (see page 46) or twisted (see page 57), and bags can be enhanced with the addition of beaded straps (see page 43).

There is a wide range of bead sizes, colours and types to choose from, but you may have difficulty threading the finer beads onto crochet yarn. If so, you need to first thread a needle with standard sewing cotton, then loop the crochet yarn through it to draw it through the bead.

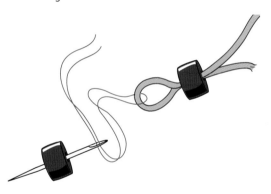

If your yarn is too thick for beads, you can make a simple twisted fringe instead (see page 56).

Pattern information

The patterns in this book are graded by skill level – easy (✪), intermediate (✪✪) and advanced (✪✪✪). Novices should select the easiest and move to the next stage after making a couple of simple projects.

The abbreviations used in these patterns are given on page 21.

Holding crochet hook

You can hold the hook in various ways, but one of the simplest and easiest methods is to hold the hook like you would a pencil, with the central shaft of the hook gripped between your thumb and forefinger as shown. If you prefer, you can hold the hook in the palm of your hand, between your thumb and first two fingers, like a knife.

When working crochet, remember to hold the base of the crochet with the first two fingers of the hand holding the yarn, as shown. This allows you to create some tension on the yarn, which is essential when pulling the hook and looped yarn through the previously made stitch.

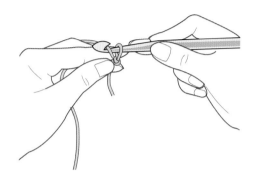

Holding yarn

You will need to be able to control the flow of yarn consistently and evenly from the ball of working yarn. One way to do this is to thread the yarn through the fingers of the left hand (if you are right-handed) as shown, with a single twist around the little finger, and with the yarn then running behind the fourth and third fingers, and over the forefinger, as shown. However, most crocheters tend to find their own working method.

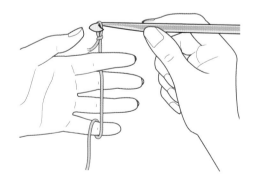

Making a loop

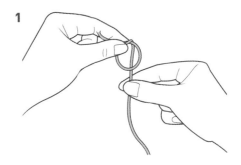

To start to crochet you need to create a first loop on the hook. There are various methods of doing this, but the one shown here is easy and quick.

1 Grasp the end of the yarn between your thumb and forefinger. Form the yarn into a loop, held in place between the thumb and the forefinger, and position the ball end of the yarn behind the loop.

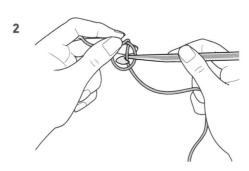

2 Holding the hook like a pencil, insert it through the centre of the loop and catch the yarn strand behind the loop with the crochet hook.

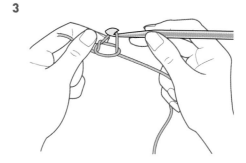

3 Draw the yarn through the loop to create a loop around the hook.

4 Pull the tail end of the yarn in the opposite direction to tighten the new loop around the hook. Do not pull the yarn too tight. The loop should slide easily on the hook.

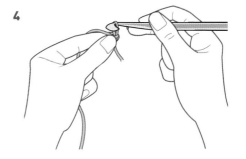

Foundation chain

To 'cast on' in crochet you will need to make a foundation chain. After you have made your first loop on the crochet hook, you then continue to make stitches as follows.

1 Catch the tail end of the yarn between your thumb and forefinger and hold it firmly.

2 Catch the ball end of the yarn with the hook, by passing the hook over and under the yarn in a twisting motion as shown by the arrow.

3 Draw the yarn now wrapped around the hook through the loop on the hook to make a chain (abbreviated in patterns as ch). Remember to hold on to the end of the chains with your other hand, to create sufficient tension as you make the stitches. Continue in this way until the required number of chains has been made (known in crochet patterns as the foundation chain).

1

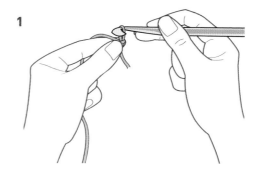

2

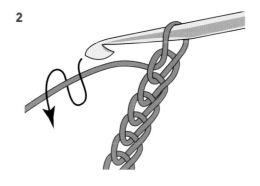

3

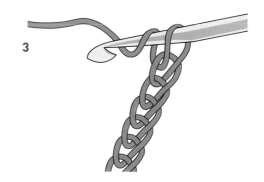

Basic stitches

Slip stitch

The shortest and easiest of the basic crochet stitches is slip stitch. On its own it forms a dense fabric, but it is usually used only as an edging or as a joining stitch.

To work a slip stitch on a foundation chain, insert the hook into the SECOND chain from the hook, catch the yarn with the hook (as shown in making a foundation chain) and draw the yarn through the chain and the loop on the hook to complete the stitch.

Working basic stitches in rows

When you turn your crochet work at the end of a row, in order to start the next row you will need to add a specific number of chain stitches – called 'turning chains' – to bring the work into the right position to create the stitches for the next row. The chart below gives the number of turning chains required for the various basic crochet stitches.

The turning chains used for treble crochet and taller stitches usually count as the first stitch in the row.

TURNING CHAINS
slip stitch – 1ch
double crochet – 1ch
half treble – 2ch
treble – 3ch
double treble – 4ch
triple treble – 5ch
quadruple treble – 6ch
quintuple treble – 7ch

Fastening off

To fasten off a piece of crochet when it is complete, first cut the thread about 7cm (3in) from the work. Then pass the loose end through the one remaining loop on the hook, and pull tightly. Darn the loose ends into on the wrong side of the work, using a blunt-ended yarn needle.

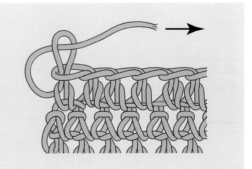

Double crochet

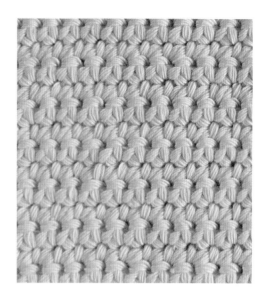

1

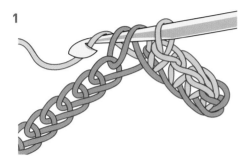

2

3

Double crochet is the most commonly used stitch in crochet and is abbreviated in patterns as dc. It creates a dense, hard-wearing textile, ideal for mats, bags or containers. It is sometimes known as 'plain stitch'. In fact, the very plain nature of the stitch is also one of its most attractive features.

How to work double crochet

1 Make a foundation chain (see page 14), then insert the hook through the SECOND chain from the hook and catch the yarn with the hook (known as yarn round hook or yrh).

2 Draw the hook through the chain so that there are now two loops on the hook.

3 Wrap the yarn around the hook and draw it through the two loops on the hook – one loop remains on the hook. Work a double crochet in each chain in the same way. On the following rows, work the one turning chain (see page 15), then work one double crochet in each stitch of the previous row.

Half trebles

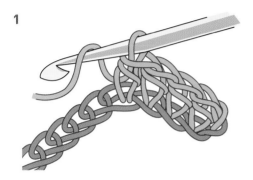

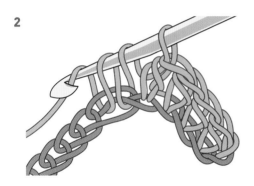

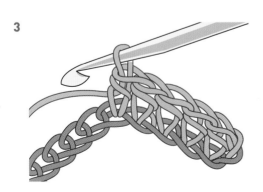

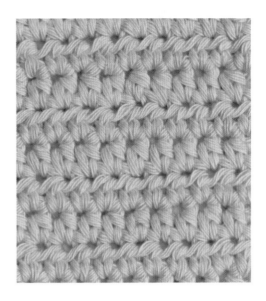

Half treble is abbreviated as htr in patterns. It is made in a similar way to double crochet but an additional twist of yarn is made around the hook before the stitch is started. This creates a slightly less dense and more flexible fabric than double crochet.

How to work half trebles

1 Make a foundation chain, then wrap the yarn around the hook and insert the hook through the THIRD chain from the hook.

2 Wrap the yarn around the hook and draw it through the chain so that there are now three loops on the hook.

3 Wrap the yarn around the hook again and draw it through all three loops to complete the stitch. Work a half treble in each chain. To start the following rows, first work the two turning chains, then miss the first stitch and work one stitch in each of the remaining stitches of the previous row, working the last stitch in the top of the turning chain.

Treble crochet

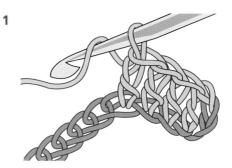

Trebles are taller than half trebles and produce a more airy-looking fabric that is softer than either double or half treble crochet. It is often used for lacy garments and household items.

How to work treble crochet

1 Yrh and insert the hook through the FOURTH chain from the hook. Yrh and draw the yarn through the chain.

2 Yrh and draw the yarn through the first two loops on the hook.

3 Yrh and draw the yarn through the two remaining loops on the hook.

4 One loop remains on the hook. Work a treble in each chain in the same way. Work the following rows as for half trebles, but make three turning chains.

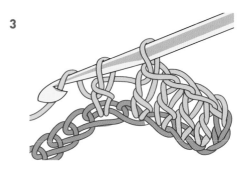

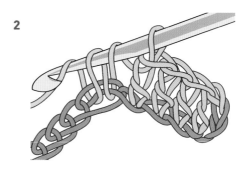

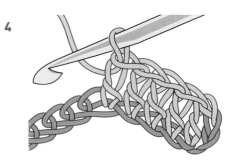

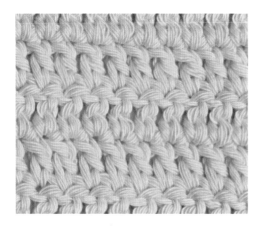

Double trebles

This is worked as for treble crochet, except that the yarn is wrapped twice around the hook before starting each stitch and four turning chains are used in subsequent rows.

Yrh twice and insert the hook in the FIFTH chain from the hook. Yrh and draw a loop through the chain – four loops are now on the hook. *Yrh and draw through two loops on the hook. Repeat from * twice more – the stitch is completed and one loop remains on the hook. Work a double treble in each chain in the same way.

Triple trebles

In this stitch (and the taller quadruple and quintuple trebles), the stitch is begun with three (or four or five) yarn wraps, and the loops are worked off the hook two at a time until one loops remains, in exactly the same way as for trebles and double trebles. A stitch is worked in each chain, then on the subsequent rows a turning chain is worked to count as the first stitch of the row (see page 15).

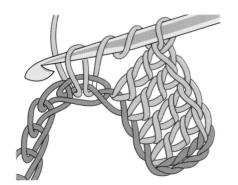
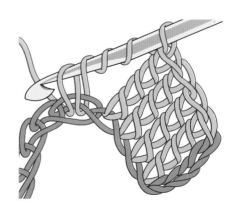

Tension

To ensure that you are working to the right measurements, and that the finished project will be the required size, you need to check the tension of the fabric you create against the tension given at the beginning of each pattern. This is indicated as rows and stitches over a 10cm (4in) block of crochet worked in the main pattern stitch of the project.

To check your tension, crochet a 13cm (5in) sample using the hook size and yarn specified, and then measure off the rows and stitches as shown below.

If your tension is too loose (fewer stitches and rows than that specified), use a finer hook. If it is too tight (more stitches and rows than that of the pattern), use a larger hook.

For some projects the final size is not particularly important: when making a blanket, for example. In this case, obtaining the correct tension is not critical. However, if you wish to ensure that a cushion cover is the right size for an existing cushion pad, for example, you will need to work to the correct tension (as you do if making fitted crochet garments).

The tension square shown right is worked in double crochet in a lightweight cotton yarn. When measuring your gauge, mark out 4in (10cm) on the sample and measure the number of rows (vertically) and the number of stitches (horizontally).

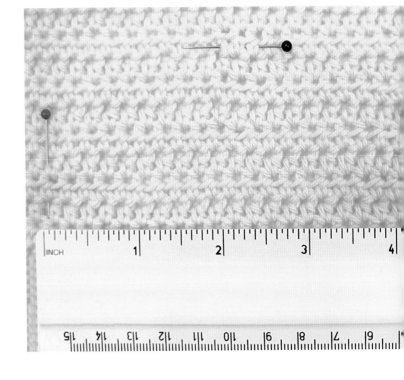

Working from patterns

Crochet abbreviations

Here are the standard abbreviations used for UK crochet patterns. Most of them are used in the patterns in this book and others are here in case you come across them in other books.

ABBREVIATIONS FOR CROCHET STITCHES

ch	chain(s)
dc	double crochet
dtr	double treble
htr	half treble
qtr	quadruple treble
quintr	quintuple treble
ss	slip stitch
tr	treble
trtr	triple treble

GENERAL CROCHET ABBREVIATIONS

alt	alternate
approx	approximately
beg	begin(ning)
blk(s)	block(s)
ch sp	chain space
CC	contrasting colour
cm	centimetre(s)
cont	continu(e)(ing)
dec	decreas(e)(ing)
foll	follow(s)(ing)
g	gram(s)
in	inch(es)
inc	increas(e)(ing)
lp(s)	loop(s)
m	metre(s)
MC	main colour
mm	millimetre(s)
oz	ounce(s)
patt(s)	pattern(s)

rem	remain(s)(ing)
rep	repeat(s)(ing)
rnd(s)	round(s)
RS	right side
sp(s)	space(s)
st(s)	stitch(es)
t-ch	turning chain
tog	together
WS	wrong side
yd	yard(s)
yrh	yarn round hook

* Repeat instructions after asterisk or between asterisks as many times as instructed.
[ ] ( ) Repeat instructions inside square brackets or parentheses as many times as instructed.

Crochet terminology

Crochet terminology is different in the UK and US, so if you buy a book when abroad it is helpful to note the differences. This book is written with UK terminology. The US equivalents are given below:

UK	US
double crochet (dc)	single crochet (sc)
half treble crochet (htr)	half double crochet (hdc)
treble crochet (tr)	double crochet (dc)
double treble (dtr)	triple (tr)
triple treble (trtr)	double treble (dtr)
quadruple treble (qtr)	triple treble (trtr)
quintuple treble (quintr)	quardruple treble (qtr)
yarn round hook (yrh)	yarn over hook (yo)
miss	skip
slip stitch (ss)	slip stitch (sl st)

Working in rounds

If you want to create a piece of crochet fabric that is circular, such as a round table mat or the base of a bag, you will have to start with a chain circle. This is created quite simply from a suitable length of foundation chains that are then linked end to end to form a ring.

1 Make a foundation chain (see page 14) of the appropriate number of chains, in this case six. Insert the hook into the first chain worked and catch the yarn with hook.

2 Draw the yarn through both the chain and the loop on the hook to join the length of chains into a circle – this is called 'join with a slip stitch'.

3 The first 'round' of the crochet is worked into the ring. The instructions in your pattern for 'round 1' will tell you what stitches and how many to work – here double crochet stitches are being worked into the ring. In the following rounds stitches are increased by working twice into the same stitch where instructed. The work is not turned at the end of rounds, so the right side of the crochet is always facing you.

This little crochet circle is the jug cover on pages 52–53. It is worked in the round, starting from a foundation chain of 6ch, which is joined with a slip stitch to create the ring. The following rounds are worked in trebles, then chain loops with picots.

1

2

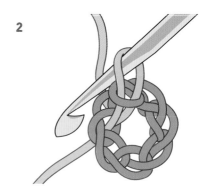

3

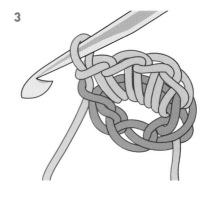

Working filet crochet

Filet crochet creates an airy texture with neatly spaced geometric holes (referred to as spaces); the connecting stitches are referred to as bars and the filled in spaces are called blocks.

Filet crochet is ideal for net edgings for pillows and hand towels, or for geometric-style projects. Traditionally worked in fine white cotton, filet crochet can be worked instead in brightly coloured crochet cottons for contemporary-looking projects.

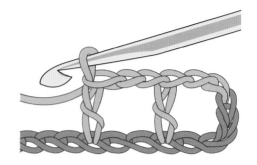

Making spaces

Making spaces
These are abbreviated as sp or sps.

To make a row of spaces, work 1tr in the 8th ch from the hook, then *work 2ch, miss 2ch, work 1tr in next chain. Repeat from * to end of chain.

Block and space
These are referred to in patterns as block (blk) and space (sp).

Work 1tr in 4th chain from hook, 1tr into each of next 2ch, *2ch, miss 2ch, 1tr in each of next 4ch. Repeat from *.

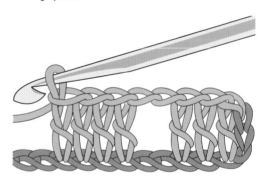

Block and space

Bar and lacet
Bars and lacets are sometimes used in combination with basic filet patterns.

To make a bar, work 5ch, miss 5 stitches or a lacet, 1tr in next stitch. To make a lacet, work 3ch, miss 2 stitches, 1dc in next stitch, 3ch, miss 2 stitches, 1 tr in to next stitch.

Bar and lacet

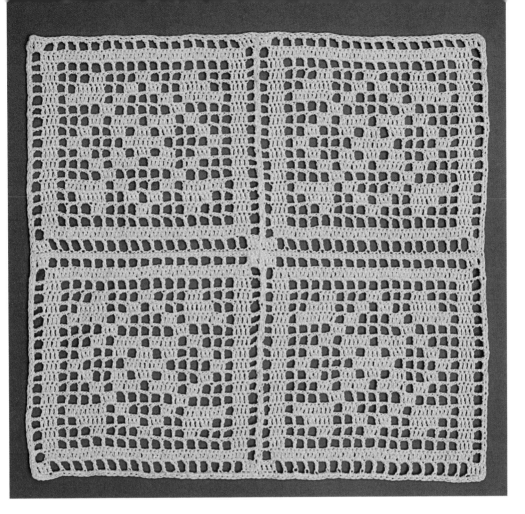

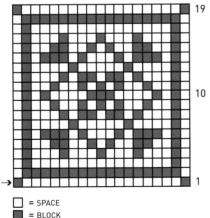

= SPACE

= BLOCK

Four individual filet squares are stitched together to form the centre decoration for the crochet cushion on pages 68–69.

Filet pillow chart

Instructions for filet crochet usually start with an explanation of how to make 'spaces' and 'blocks' and written instructions for the first few rows. Then a chart, similar to the chart here for the Filet Pillow on page 68, is followed with ease for the remaining rows.

Simple crochet edgings

You can use the edgings shown here for pillows, towels, cushions, collars and cuffs, for example. All these edgings are made on a foundation chain slightly longer than the desired length of the edging, except for the Fan Edging. You can use fine crochet threads for them, as on towel and pillow edgings on pages 66–67 and 70–71, or a lightweight cotton yarn, as used here for these samples, for garments.

If you like, you can make a sample swatch of your edging first to work out precisely how many chain stitches to start with.

After finishing any edgings, pin out and press them lightly, then stitch to the crocheted, knitted or fabric item.

To make loop edging

To begin, make a foundation chain slightly longer than the desired length of the edging. The number of chains must be a multiple of 4, plus 2 extra.

Row 1 (WS) 1dc in 2nd ch from hook, 1dc in each of rem ch. Turn.

Row 2 (RS) 3ch, miss first 2dc, 1tr in next dc, 5ch, *1tr in same dc as last tr, (miss next dc, 1tr in next dc) twice, 5ch; rep from * to last 2dc, 1tr in same dc as last tr, miss next dc, 1tr in last dc.
Fasten off.

To make scallop edging

To begin, make a foundation chain slightly longer than the desired length of the edging. The number of chains must be a multiple of 6, plus 2 extra.

Row 1 (WS) 1dc in 2nd ch from hook, 1dc in each of rem ch. Turn.

Row 2 (RS) 1ch, 1dc in first dc, *miss next 2dc, 7dtr in next dc, miss next 2dc, 1dc in next dc; rep from * to end.
Fasten off.

To make cluster edging

To begin, make a foundation chain slightly longer than the desired length of the edging. The number of chains must be a multiple of 6, plus 2 extra.

Row 1 (WS) 1dc in 2nd ch from hook, 1dc in each of rem ch. Turn.

Row 2 (RS) 4ch, then leaving last loop of each dtr on hook, work 2dtr in first dc, yrh and draw a loop through all 3 loops on hook (2dtr-cluster made), *8ch, 1dc in 3rd ch from hook (picot made), 5ch, then leaving last loop of each dtr on hook, work 3dtr in same dc as last cluster, yrh and draw a loop through all 4 loops on hook (3dtr-cluster made), miss next 5dc, 3dtr-cluster in next dc; rep from * to end, omitting 3dtr-cluster at end of last rep. Fasten off.

To make fan edging

To begin, make 12ch.

Row 1 (WS) 1dc in 8th ch from hook, 5ch, miss next 3ch, work (1tr, 3ch, 1tr) all in next ch. Turn.

Row 2 (RS) 3ch, 9tr in 3-ch sp, 1dc in 5-ch loop, 5ch, 1dc in 7-ch loop at end. Turn.

Row 3 7ch, 1dc in 5-ch loop, 5ch, work (1tr, 3ch, 1tr) all in 5th tr (centre tr) of 9tr group. Turn.

Rep rows 2 and 3 until edging is desired
length, ending with a row 2.
Fasten off.

To make Venetian edging

To begin, make a foundation chain slightly
longer than the desired length of the edging.
The number of chains must be a multiple of
5, plus 2 extra.

Row 1 (WS) 1dc in 2nd ch from hook, 1dc in
each of rem ch. Turn.

Row 2 (RS) 6ch, 1tr in first dc, *(miss next
dc, 1tr in next dc) twice, 3ch, 1tr in next dc;
rep from * to end. Turn.

Row 3 1ch, work (1dc, 3ch, 1dc) all in first 3-
ch sp, *5ch, work (1dc, 3ch, 1dc) all in next
3-ch sp; rep from *, working last (1dc, 3ch,
1dc) all in 6-ch loop at end. Turn.

Row 4 1ch, 1dc in first 3-ch loop, *4ch, 1dtr
in next 5-ch loop, 4ch, 1dc in next 3-ch loop;
rep from * to end. Turn.

Row 5 5dc in first 4-ch loop, *5ch, 5dc in
each of next 2 4-ch loops; rep from *, ending
with 5dc in last 4-ch loop.
Fasten off.

To make double-picot edging

To begin, make a foundation chain slightly
longer than the desired length of the edging.
The number of chains must be a multiple of
7, plus 6 extra.

Row 1 (RS) 1dc in 2nd ch from hook, 1dc in
each of next 2ch, *4ch and work 1dc in 4rd
ch from hook – called *make picot* – , 1dc in
each of next 2ch, turn, 9ch, 1dc in 3rd dc
before picot, turn, work (5dc, make picot,
3dc, make picot, 5dc) all in 9-ch loop, 1dc in
each of next 5ch; rep from * to end, omitting
5dc at end of last rep.
Fasten off.

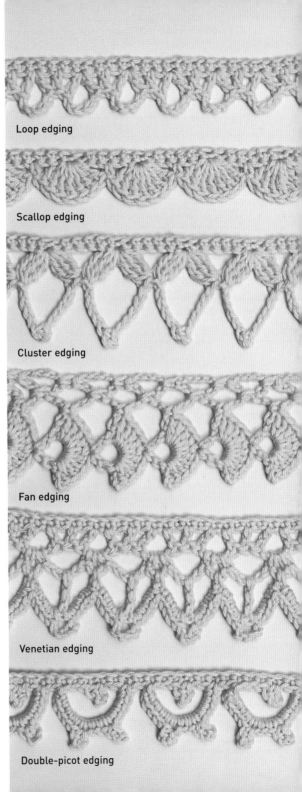

Loop edging

Scallop edging

Cluster edging

Fan edging

Venetian edging

Double-picot edging

gallery of projects

Double-crochet pot holder

✪ *Crocheted in easy-to-work double crochet, the two layers of this pot holder are joined with a picot edging. Make your own stripes to suit.*

You will need
- *Coats Lyric 8/8* medium-weight cotton yarn:
    2 x 50g balls in main colour (**MC**) – purple (shade no. 5028)
    1 x 50g ball in contrasting colour (**CC**) – orange (shade no.5037)
- 3.00mm (US D-3), 4.00mm (US G-6) and 4.50mm (US 7) crochet hooks
- Small metal or plastic ring

Tension and finished size
- 17 stitches and 19 rows to 10cm (4in) over dc using 4.00mm (US G-6) hook.
- Pot holder measures 18cm (7in) square, excluding edging.

To make pot holder
The pot holder has a back and front. The back forms a pocket into which you can slip your hand, or for really hot things you can use the double thickness.

FRONT
To begin, using 4.50mm (US 7) hook and MC, make 29ch.
Change to 4.00mm (US G-6) hook and cont.
Row 1 (RS) 1dc in 2nd ch from hook, 1dc in each of rem ch. Turn. (28dc)
Row 2 1ch, 1dc in first dc, 1dc in each dc to last dc, 1dc in last dc changing to CC with last yrh of st. Turn.
Rep row 2 28 times more **and at the same time** work stripe sequence as foll, changing to new colour with last yrh of previous row: 1 row CC, 7 rows MC, 1 row CC, 9 rows MC, 1 row CC, 5 rows MC, 1 row CC***, 3 rows MC. Fasten off.

BACK
Work as for front to ***.
Using 3.00mm (US D-3) hook and MC, work one row more in dc.
Fasten off.

EDGING
Round 1 Using 3.00mm (US D-3) hook and MC and holding front and back with wrong sides tog and foundation-chain edges aligned, insert hook through edge of both layers of pot holder at centre of one side, yrh and draw yarn through, work 1ch, 1dc in same place ch was worked, then work dc evenly around edge of pot holder, working 3dc in each corner and working edging at top through the front only; finish by joining with a ss in first dc. (Do not turn at end of rounds.)
Round 2 1ch, 1dc in same place as ss, 1dc in each of next 2dc, *3ch, ss in last dc worked (one picot made), 1dc in each of next 3dc; rep from * around pot holder, but work 3dc in each corner, leave one corner at top free of picots for attaching hanging ring and adjust space between last two picots as necessary to fit; finish by joining with a ss in first dc. Fasten off.

To finish
Press. Weave in any loose ends.
Using 3.00mm (US D-3) hook and MC, work dc around the ring and join with a ss to first dc. Fasten off. Stitch to corner of pot holder.

Simple blanket

✪ *This blanket can be made in two sizes – a baby blanket size and an afghan size. It is worked in double crochet and chain stitches, which creates a soft, supple fabric. Make up your own striped version if you wish.*

You will need
- *Coats Lyric 8/8* medium-weight cotton yarn:
    12 [**23**] x 50g balls in main colour (**MC**) – green (shade no. 5089)
    2 [**2**] x 50g balls in first contrasting colour (**A**) – turquoise (shade no. 5090)
    1 [**1**] x 50g ball in second contrasting colour (**B**) – pale blue (shade no. 5010)
    1 [**1**] x 50g ball in second contrasting colour (**C**) – lime (shade no. 5057)
- 5.50mm (US I-9) and 6.00mm (US J-10) crochet hooks

Tension and finished size
- 20 stitches (10dc and 10 1-ch sps) and 14 rows to 10cm (4in) over pattern stitch using 5.50mm (US I-9) hook.
- Blanket measures 97 [**120**]cm x 97 [**148**]cm (38¾ [**48**]in x 38¾ [**58**]in), including border

Special note
If desired, you can change the size of the blanket. Figure out how many stitches are needed across the row by using the tension given above. Make one foundation chain for each stitch needed, plus one extra. If the number of stitches is even, add one more chain to make it an odd number – the pattern requires an odd number of foundation chains.

To make blanket
To begin, using 6.00mm (US J-10) hook and MC, make 185 [**231**]ch.
Change to 5.50mm (US I-9) hook and cont.
Row 1 1dc in 2nd ch from hook, *1ch, miss next ch, 1dc in next ch; rep from * to last ch, 1dc in last ch. Turn.
Row 2 1ch, 1dc in first dc, 1ch, 1dc in next 1-ch sp; rep from * to last dc, 1dc in last dc. Turn.
Rep row 2 to form patt st until blanket measures 92cm (36in) from beg **and at the same time** work in stripe sequence as foll: 3 rows more in MC, 1 row A, 1 row B, 7 rows MC, 1 row C, 1 row A, 14 rows MC, 1 row C, 22 rows MC, 1 row A, 31 [**101**] rows MC, 1 row A, 1 row B, 3 rows MC, 1 row C, 1 row A, 17 rows MC, 1 row C, 9 rows MC, 1 row C, 1 row A, 8 rows MC.
Note: If necessary, stop stripe sequence when blanket measures 92 [**115**]cm (36¾ [**46**]in) from beg (and end with one row MC), or if sequence is complete, cont with MC only until it reaches this length.
Fasten off.
BORDER
Round 1 Using 5.50mm (US I-9) hook and MC, insert hook through edge of blanket at any corner, yrh and draw yarn through, work 1ch, 1dc in same place as ch was worked; then work dc evenly around edge of blanket, working 3dc in each corner, and join with a ss in first dc. (Do not turn at end of rounds but work with same side always facing.)
Round 2 3ch, then working into back loop only of dc of previous round, work 1tr in each

dc all around edge, except work 3tr in each corner dc, and join with a ss to 3rd of first 3ch. Fasten off.

Round 3 Using A (turquoise), insert hook through a tr, yrh and draw yarn through, work 1ch; then working into back loop only of tr of previous round, work 1dc same place as ch was worked and 1dc in each tr all around edge, except work 3dc in each corner tr, and join with a ss to first dc.

Fasten off.

Weave in any loose ends.

Circular cushion

✪✪ *You can make this circular cushion with or without its flower motif adornment (see pages 36 and 37). Make several in different toning colours. It is easy to work once you master the art of working in rounds (see page 22). You could also add a simple picot edging (see pages 26–27) to the cushion in a contrasting colour, if you prefer.*

You will need
- *Patons Diploma Gold DK* wool-mix double-knitting weight yarn:
  3 x 50g balls in main colour (**MC**) – taupe (shade no. 06237)
  Small amount in first contrasting colour (**A**) – cream (shade no. 06142)
  Small amount in second contrasting colour (**B**) – natural (shade no. 06143)
  Small amount in third contrasting colour (**C**) – cayenne (shade no. 06304)
- 4.00mm (US G-6) crochet hook
- Cushion pad to fit

Tension and finished size
- 18 stitches and 9 rows to 10cm (4in) over treble crochet using 4.00mm (US G-6) hook.
- Finished cushion measures approximately 38cm (15in) in diameter.

To make cushion cover
The cushion cover is made from two identical pieces.

FRONT AND BACK (BOTH ALIKE)
To begin, using MC make 4ch and join with a ss in first ch to form a ring.

Round 1 (RS) 3ch (these 3ch at beg of rounds count as first tr), 11tr in ring, 1ss in 3rd of first 3ch. Do not turn at end of rounds, but work with RS always facing. (12 sts)

Round 2 3ch, 1tr in same place as ss, 2tr in each of rem tr, 1ss in 3rd of first 3ch. (24 sts)

Round 3 3ch, 1tr in same place as ss, *1tr in next tr, 2tr in each of next 2tr; rep from * to last 2tr, 1tr in next tr, 2tr in last tr, 1ss in 3rd of first 3ch. (40 sts)

Round 4 3ch, 1tr in same place as ss, *1tr in each of next 3tr, 2tr in next tr; rep from * to last 3tr, 1tr in each of last 3tr, 1ss in 3rd of first 3ch. (50 sts)

Round 5 3ch, 1tr in same place as ss, *1tr in each of next 4tr, 2tr in next tr; rep from * to last 4tr, 1tr in each of last 4tr, 1ss in 3rd of first 3ch. (60 sts)

Round 6 3ch, 1tr in same place as ss, *1tr in each of next 5tr, 2tr in next tr; rep from * to last 5tr, 1tr in each of last 5tr, 1ss in 3rd of first 3ch. (70 sts)

Round 7 3ch, 1tr in same place as ss, *1tr in each of next 6tr, 2tr in next tr; rep from * to last 6tr, 1tr in each of last 6tr, 1ss in 3rd of first 3ch. (80 sts)

Round 8 3ch, 1tr in same place as ss, *1tr in each of next 7tr, 2tr in next tr; rep from * to last 7tr, 1tr in each of last 7tr, 1ss in 3rd of first 3ch. (90 sts)

Round 9 3ch, 1tr in same place as ss, *1tr in each of next 8tr, 2tr in next tr; rep from * to last 8tr, 1tr in each of last 8tr, 1ss in 3rd of first 3ch. (100 sts)

Round 10 As round 5. (120 sts)

Round 11 3ch, 1tr in same place as ss, *1tr

in each of next 11tr, 2tr in next tr; rep from *
to last 11tr, 1tr in each of last 11tr, 1ss in 3rd
of first 3ch. (130 sts)
Round 12 3ch, 1tr in same place as ss, *1tr
in each of next 12tr, 2tr in next tr; rep from *
to last 12tr, 1tr in each of last 12tr, 1ss in 3rd
of first 3ch. (140 sts)
Round 13 As round 7. (160 sts)
Round 14 3ch, 1tr in same place as ss, *1tr
in each of next 15tr, 2tr in next tr; rep from *
to last 15tr, 1tr in each of last 15tr, 1ss in 3rd
of first 3ch. (170 sts)
Round 15 3ch, 1tr in same place as ss, *1tr
in each of next 16tr, 2tr in next tr; rep from *
to last 16tr, 1tr in each of last 16tr, 1ss in 3rd
of first 3ch. (180 sts)
Round 16 3ch, 1tr in same place as ss, *1tr
in each of next 17tr, 2tr in next tr; rep from *
to last 17tr, 1tr in each of last 17tr, 1ss in 3rd
of first 3ch. (190 sts)
Round 17 3ch, 1tr in same place as ss, *1tr
in each of next 18tr, 2tr in next tr; rep from *
to last 18tr, 1tr in each of last 18tr, 1ss in 3rd
of first 3ch. (200 sts)
Fasten off.
FLOWER MOTIF
To begin, using B make 4ch and join with a ss
in first ch to form a ring.
Round 1 (RS) 6dc in ring. Do not turn at end
of rounds, but work with RS always facing.
Round 2 2dc in each dc. (12 sts)
Then working into back loop only of each dc,
cont in a spiral as foll:
(2dc in next dc, 1dc in next dc) 15 times, (2dc
in next dc, 1dc in each of next 2dc) 9 times,
(2dc in next dc, 1dc in each of next 3dc) 10
times, 1dc in next dc.
Fasten off.
Starting in first unworked front loop of dc
near centre of flower, add petals as foll:
Using A, (1ss in next dc, 2tr in each of next
3dc, 1ss in next dc) 6 times.

Using B, (1ss in next dc, 2tr in each of next
3dc, 1ss in next dc) 6 times.
Using C, (1ss in next dc, 2tr in each of next
3dc, 1ss in next dc) 17 times.
Fasten off.

To finish
Press the front and back of the cushion
lightly on WS with a cool iron following the
instructions on the yarn label.
Sew flower motif to centre of front.
EDGING
Place cushion pad between back and front
and join front and back by working dc around
the edge through both layers, using MC.
Fasten off.

Adding one crocheted flower to the centre of the
front of the cushion adds an interesting detail. The
flower motif is worked round and round in a spiral
and is great fun to make.

Striped cushions

✪ *You have an alternative design for this simple blocks and stripes cushion. The version shown opposite is the main pattern, but a simpler version is given on page 40. You can, if you wish, make the cushion front in one pattern and the reverse in the other.*

You could adapt the design to make a simple throw, too, increasing the quantities of yarn proportionally and picking your own colourways to suit your decor.

You will need
- *Patons Diploma Gold DK* wool-mix double-knitting weight yarn for each cushion:
   4 x 50g balls in **A** – steel grey (shade no. 06184)
   4 x 50g balls in **B** – white (shade no. 06187)
- 4.00mm (US G-6) crochet hook
- Cushion pad to fit

Tension and finished size
- 19 stitches and 14 rows to 10cm (4in) over striped pattern stitch using 4.00mm (US G-6) hook.
- Each version of the finished cushion measures 46cm (18¼in) square.

Special note
When changing colours for stripes, change to new colour with last yrh of last dc of previous row.

To make strips version
The front and back of the cushion are each made from four strips. Keep track of which strip is which so they can be joined in the correct sequence when complete.

STRIP 1 (MAKE 2)
To begin, using A make 24ch.
Beg patt as foll:
Row 1 (RS) 1tr in 4th ch from hook, 1tr in each of rem ch. Turn.
Row 2 1ch, 1dc in each tr, 1dc in 3rd of 3ch. Turn. (22dc)
Row 3 3ch to count as first tr, miss first dc, *1tr in next dc; rep from * to end.
Row 4 1ch, 1dc in each tr, 1dc in 3rd of 3ch. Turn.
Rep rows 3–4 to form patt st.
Cont in patt (of one row tr and one row dc alternately) **and at the same time** work in stripes as foll:
12 more rows A, (2 rows B, 2 rows A) 4 times, 16 rows B, (2 rows A, 2 rows B) 4 times.
Fasten off.
STRIP 2 (MAKE 2)
Work as for Strip 1, but in stripe sequence as foll:
(2 rows A, 2 rows B) 4 times times, 16 rows A, (2 rows B, 2 rows A) 4 times, 16 rows B.
Fasten off.
STRIP 3 (MAKE 2)
Work as for Strip 1, but in stripe sequence as foll:
16 rows B, (2 rows A, 2 rows B) 4 times, 16 rows A, (2 rows B, 2 rows A) 4 times.
Fasten off.
STRIP 4 (MAKE 2)
Work as for Strip 1, but in stripe sequence as foll:
(2 rows B, 2 rows A) 4 times, 16 rows B,

(2 rows A, 2 rows B) 4 times, 16 rows A. Fasten off.

To finish

Press the strips lightly on WS with a cool iron following the instructions on the yarn label. For the cushion front, arrange the strips (with foundation-chain edges aligned) from left to right as foll:
One Strip 1, one Strip 2, one Strip 3, and one Strip 4.
Join strips in this order with a fine backstitch.
For the cushion back, arrange the strips (with foundation-chain edges aligned) from left to right as foll:
One Strip 3, one Strip 4, one Strip 1, and one Strip 2.
Join strips in this order as for front.
Press seams lightly. With right sides together, join front to back around three sides. Turn right side out and insert cushion pad. Join opening.

To make simple stripes version

The cushion cover is made from two identical pieces.

FRONT AND BACK (BOTH ALIKE)

To begin, using A make 90ch.
Beg patt as foll:
Row 1 (RS) Using A, 1tr in 4th ch from hook, 1tr in each of rem ch. Turn.
Row 2 Using A, 1ch, 1dc in each tr, 1dc in 3rd of 3ch, changing to B with last yrh of last dc. Turn. (88dc)
Row 3 Using B, 3ch to count as first tr, miss first dc; *1tr in next dc; rep from * to end.
Row 4 Using B, 1ch, 1dc in each tr, 1dc in 3rd of 3ch, changing to A with last yrh of last dc. Turn.
Rep rows 3–4 to form patt st.
Cont in patt (of one row tr and one row dc

alternately) **and at the same time** work in stripes as foll:
(2 rows A, 2 rows B) 3 times times, 16 rows A, (2 rows B, 2 rows A) 4 times, 16 rows B. Fasten off.

To finish

Press the front and back lightly on WS with a cool iron following the instructions on the yarn label.
With right sides together, join front to back around three sides. Turn right side out and insert cushion pad. Join opening.

The simple stripes version of the cushion cover is much quicker to work, with just one piece for the front and one piece for the back. You could work a treble-crochet back in a single bright contrasting colour for an even faster project.

Colourwork bags

⭐ *Here are two styles of bag with the same basic stitch pattern. The rectangular bag (right) has a beaded chain strap, and the square bag (see page 44) has a crocheted handle.*

The bags use only double and treble crochet stitches, and the bicolour design is not difficult. You could adapt the pattern to make a little coin purse to match (which will take proportionately less yarn).

You will need

SQUARE BAG
- *Coats Lyric 8/4* lightweight cotton yarn:
    1 x 50g ball in **A** – black (shade no. 5001)
    1 x 50g ball in **B** – white (shade no. 5000)
- 5g skein of *Anchor Pearl Cotton No. 5* in red (shade no. 47), for 2 tassels
- 3.00mm (US D-3) and 3.50mm (US E-4) crochet hooks

RECTANGULAR BAG
- *Coats Lyric 8/4* lightweight cotton yarn:
    1 x 50g ball in **A** – black (shade no. 5001)
    1 x 50g ball in **B** – white (shade no. 5000)
- 30 wooden beads 7–9mm in diameter, to decorate strap
- 3.00mm (US D-3), 3.50mm (US E-4) and 4.00mm (US G-6) crochet hooks

BOTH BAGS
- Zipper 20cm (8in) long
- Lining fabric (optional)

Tension and finished size
- 22 stitches and 16 rows to 10cm (4in) over pattern stitch using 3.00mm (US D-3) hook.
- Square bag measures 20cm (8in) square.
- Rectangular bag measures 13cm (5in) tall x 20cm (8in) wide.

To make square bag
To begin, using 3.50mm (US E-4) hook and A, make 44ch. (The first row of the pattern must be worked over a multiple of 4ch.)
Change to 3.00mm (US D-3) hook and beg patt as foll:
Row 1 1dc in 2nd ch from hook, 1dc in each of rem ch. Turn. (43dc)
Row 2 1ch, 1dc in first dc, *1dc in next dc, – 4ch, 1ss in last dc worked (a picot made) – , 1dc in each of next 3dc; rep from * omitting 3dc at end of last rep, insert hook in next dc (which is last dc), yrh and draw yarn through, drop A, pick up B and draw yarn through rem 2 loops on hook (colour changed). Turn.
Row 3 (WS) 3ch, 1dc in first picot, *1tr in each of next 3 free dc, 1dc in next picot; rep from *, ending with 1tr in last dc. Turn.
Row 4 (RS) 1ch, 1dc in first tr, *1dc in next dc, 1 picot, 1dc in each of next 3tr; rep from * omitting 3dc at end of last rep, insert hook in 3rd of 3ch, yrh and draw yarn through, drop B, pick up A and draw yarn through rem 2 loops on hook (colour changed again – always change colour in this way). Turn.
Row 5 As row 3.
Row 6 As row 4, but dropping A and picking up B.**
Rep rows 3–6 to form patt.

The rectangular bag (right) has a long beaded strap. Adjust the length of the strap if desired.

Work in patt until bag measures 40cm (16in) from beg, ending with a 5th patt row (in A).
Next row 1ch, 1dc in each st.
Fasten off.

HANDLE
Using 3.50mm (US E-4) hook and A, make 61ch – for a 30cm (12in) long handle. Change to 3.00mm (US D-3) hook and make handle as foll:
Row 1 1tr in 4th ch from hook, 1tr in each of rem ch. Turn.
Row 2 3ch, miss first tr, 1tr in next tr, 1tr in each of rem tr. Turn.
Row 3 As row 2.
Fold handle in half lengthways, bringing foundation-ch edge up level with top of previous row. Then work a row of dc through foundation-ch and top of previous row, but beginning and ending 2cm (³/₄in) from end of handle.

TASSELS
Make two 7cm (2³/₄in) long tassels in C as foll:
Wind the thread about 50 times around a piece of cardboard 10cm (4in) wide. Tie one end of the loops together tightly, then cut the other end of the loops to remove the tassel from the cardboard. Bind the tassel together near the top by winding an separate length securely around it. Trim the ends.

To make rectangular bag
Work as for square bag to **.
Rep rows 3–6 to form patt.
Work in patt until bag measures 26cm (10in) from beg, ending with a 5th patt row (in A).
Next row 1ch, 1dc in each st.
Fasten off.

STRAP
Before beg cord, string 30 beads onto a ball of A so they are ready to use while crocheting strap. Then using 4.00mm (US G-6) hook and 2 strands of A held tog (one strand with beads on and another one without beads), work chain stitches, catching a bead into chain every 5–6cm (2–2¹/₂in) by sliding bead up close to work then continuing chain. Work in this way until strap is 122cm (48in) long or desired length (be sure to stretch strap when measuring). Fasten off.

To finish bags
Fold bag in half, right sides together and oversew side seams. Turn right side out.
Secure handle to square bag on outside of bag, overlapping unfolded ends over top of side seams. Secure strap to rectangular bag on inside of bag at side seams.
Backstitch zipper to opening.
Line bag with fabric if desired.
Sew a tassel to square bag below each end of handle.

The square bag on the opposite page has tassels made from a skein of pearl cotton embroidery thread, which gives it a nice sheen to contrast with the more matt finish of the bag yarn.

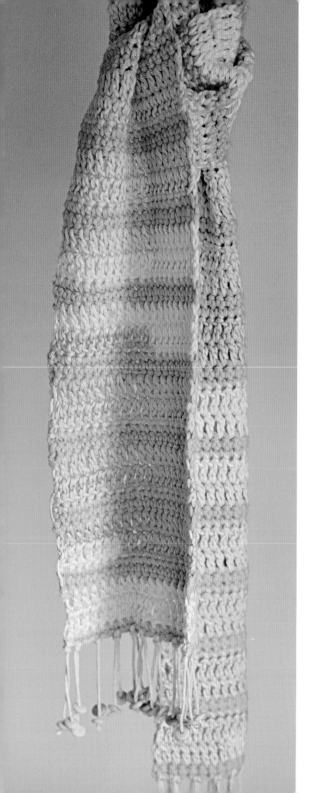

Treble-crochet scarf

✪ *This cotton scarf is made with two yarns only, despite its look. One yarn is a plain beige shade, forming intermittant stripes throughout, and the other is a random-dyed yarn in pastel blues and greens. Using a random-dyed yarn is a great way to add lots of colour to your crochet with little effort, and it comes in a variety of colours.*

The simple crochet texture is created by mixing alternating simple double crochet with treble crochet.

You will need

- 3 x 50g balls of *Anchor Magic* medium-weight cotton yarn in main colour (**MC**) – shades of blues and greens (shade no. 1430)
- 2 x 50g balls of *Coats Lyric 8/8* medium-weight cotton yarn in contrasting colour (**CC**) – beige (shade no. 5003)
- 5.50mm (US I-9) and 6.00mm (US J-10) crochet hooks
- 44 beads for fringe

Tension and finished size

- 14 stitches to 10cm (4in) over pattern using 5.50mm (US I-9) hook.
- Scarf measures 14cm (5¾in) wide x 165cm (65in) long, excluding fringe. Length is adjustable.

Special note

When working stripe pattern, drop MC at side of work when not in use and pick it up when next needed. But cut off CC after each CC stripe and rejoin when next needed, working over ends to avoid having to weave in later.

To make scarf

To begin, using 6.00mm (US J-10) hook and CC, make 21ch.

Change to 5.50mm (US I-9) hook and cont.

Row 1 Using CC, 1dc in 2nd ch from hook, 1dc in each of rem ch, changing to MC with last yrh of last dc. Turn. (20dc)

Row 2 Using MC, work 3ch to count as first tr, miss first dc, *1tr in next dc; rep from *. Turn. (20 sts)

Row 3 Using MC, 3ch, miss first tr, *1tr in next tr; rep from *, ending with 1tr in 3rd of 3ch and changing to CC with last yrh of last tr. Turn.

Row 4 Using CC, 1ch, 1dc in each tr, ending with 1dc in 3rd of 3ch. Turn. (20dc)

Row 5 Using CC, 1ch, 1dc in each dc, changing to MC with last yrh of last dc. Turn. Rep rows 2–5 to form stripe patt. Work in stripe patt until scarf measures 165cm (65in) or desired length, ending with a row 4. Fasten off.

BEADED FRINGE

For fringe cut 22 lengths of MC, each 20cm (8in) long. Thread two beads onto each length of MC and knot each end to hold on beads, placing knots about 9cm (3¹/₂in) apart. Trim yarn ends close to knots. Slide one bead up close to each knot.

Attach 11 beaded strands evenly spaced along each end of scarf. To do this, fold a beaded strand in half, then insert hook through edge of scarf and draw the loop at the fold through. Pass the beaded ends through the loop and pull tight to secure.

Choose lightweight beads like these, to make the scarf comfortable and easy to wear. You'll find that bead details are real eyecatchers.

String bag

✪✪ *This adaptable little shopping bag stretches when filled. It is smartly trimmed with jazzy glass beads. An adaptation of the lacy, circular pattern makes a pretty jug cover or a little mat (see page 51 for instructions).*

You will need
- 1 x 50g ball of *Coats Aida No. 10* cotton crochet thread or of *Coats Eldorado* cotton crochet thread in chosen colour
- 1.50mm (US 6 steel) crochet hook
- 12 beads to decorate ends of cords (optional)

Tension and finished size
- First 4 rounds of treble crochet measure 5cm (2in) in diameter using 1.50mm (US 6 steel) hook.
- Bag is approximately 35cm (13¾in) deep, but stretches when filled.

To make string bag
To begin, make 6ch and join with a ss in first ch to form a ring.

Round 1 (RS) 3ch (these 3ch at beg of tr rounds count as first tr), 11tr in ring, 1ss in 3rd of first 3ch. Do not turn at end of rounds, but work with RS always facing. (12 sts)

Round 2 3ch, 1tr in same place as ss, 2tr in each of rem tr, 1ss in 3rd of first 3ch. (24 sts)

Round 3 As round 2. (48 sts)

Round 4 3ch, 1tr in each tr, 1ss in 3rd of first 3ch.

Round 5 3ch, 1tr in same place as ss, *1tr in next tr, 2tr in next tr; rep from *, ending with 1tr in last tr, 1ss in 3rd of first 3ch. (72 sts)

Round 6 3ch, 1tr in same place as ss, *1tr in each of next 2tr, 2tr in next tr; rep from *, ending with 1tr in each of last 2tr, 1ss in 3rd of first 3ch. (96 sts)

Round 7 As round 4.

Round 8 3ch, 1tr in same place as ss, *1tr in each of next 3tr, 2tr in next tr; rep from *, ending with 1tr in each of last 3tr, 1ss in 3rd of first 3ch. (120 sts)

Round 9 1ch, 1dc in same place as ss, *3ch, 1dc in next tr, 5ch, miss next 2tr, 1dc in next tr; rep from *, ending with 3ch, 1dc in next tr, 2ch, 1tr in first dc.

Round 10 Work (1dc, 3ch, 1dc) all in loop just formed with 2ch and 1tr, *5ch, (1dc, 3ch, 1dc) all in next 5-ch loop; rep from *, ending with 2ch, 1tr in first dc. (30 loops, including last loop formed with 2ch and 1tr)

Round 11 Work (1dc, 3ch, 1dc) all in loop just formed, *6ch, (1dc, 3ch, 1dc) all in next 5-ch loop; rep from *, ending with 2ch, 1dtr in first dc.

Round 12 Work (1dc, 3ch, 1dc) all in loop just formed, *7ch, (1dc, 3ch, 1dc) all in next 6-ch loop; rep from *, ending with 3ch, 1dtr in first dc.

Round 13 Work (1dc, 3ch, 1dc) all in loop just formed, *8ch, (1dc, 3ch, 1dc) all in next 7-ch loop; rep from *, ending with 3ch, 1trtr in first dc.

Round 14 Work (1dc, 3ch, 1dc) all in loop just formed, *9ch, (1dc, 3ch, 1dc) all in next 8-ch loop; rep from *, ending with 4ch, 1trtr in first dc.

Round 15 Work (1dc, 3ch, 1dc) all in loop just formed, *10ch, (1dc, 3ch, 1dc) all in next 9-ch

loop; rep from *, ending with 4ch, 1qtr in first dc.

Round 16 Work (1dc, 3ch, 1dc) all in loop just formed, *11ch, (1dc, 3ch, 1dc) all in next 10-ch loop; rep from *, ending with 5ch, 1qtr in first dc.

Round 17 Work (1dc, 3ch, 1dc) all in loop just formed, *12ch, (1dc, 3ch, 1dc) all in next 11-ch loop; rep from *, ending with 5ch, 1quintr in first dc.

Round 18 Work (1dc, 3ch, 1dc) all in loop just formed, *13ch, (1dc, 3ch, 1dc) all in next 12-ch loop; rep from *, ending with 6ch, 1quintr in first dc.

Round 19 Work (1dc, 3ch, 1dc) all in loop just formed, *13ch, (1dc, 3ch, 1dc) all in next 13-ch loop; rep from *, ending with 6ch, 1quintr in first dc.

Rep 19th round 18 times more.

Next round 1dc in loop just formed, *9ch, 1dc in next 13-ch loop; rep from *, ending with 9ch, 1ss in first dc.

Next round 3ch, *1tr in each of next 9ch, 1tr in next dc; rep from * omitting 1tr at end of last rep, 1ss in 3rd of first 3ch.

Next round 1ch, 1dc in same place as ss, *3ch, 1dc in each of next 5tr; rep from * omitting 1dc at end of last rep, 1ss in first dc. Fasten off.

CORD HANDLES

Make two cords for the handles of the string bag, each 87cm (34in) long. For an extra-simple cord, make a foundation chain and work one row of double crochet. For the attractive cord shown, using the step-by-step illustrations for guidance, work each of the cords as foll:

To begin, make 2ch loosely, then work 1dc in the first ch made (**step 1**), turn, 1dc in foundation loop of 2nd ch made inserting hook in back of loop (**step 2**), *turn, insert hook in 2 loops at side (**step 3**), yrh and draw

loop through, yrh and draw through 2 loops on hook; rep from * for length required. Fasten off.

To finish

Thread cords alternately through last picot row of bag. Tie ends of each cord together and decorate 4 ends with beads as desired.

1

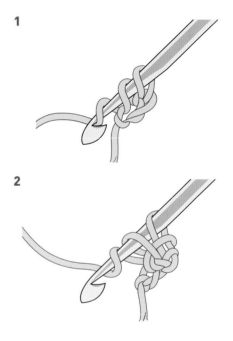

2

3

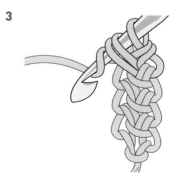

Traditional jug cover

You can adapt the bag pattern to make a traditional beaded jug cover. It only takes one 50g ball of *Coats Aida No. 10* crochet cotton (or one ball of *Coats Eldorado* crochet cotton) and a total of 30 glass beads (twenty 7mm round beads and ten larger beads – the larger ones used here are tubular and measure 9mm in diameter and 10mm long). Make sure the beads you buy have large enough holes for the crochet thread.

TO MAKE JUG COVER

Before beginning, thread 30 beads onto the crochet thread in reverse order so they are ready to use in the last round. *Thread on two small beads, one large bead; repeat from * until they are all on.

To begin the jug cover, work rounds 1–13 of the pattern for the string bag.

Then work the final round as foll:

Round 14 (bead round) Work (1dc, 3ch, 1dc) all in loop just formed, *7ch, slide a large bead up close to the hook and make 1ch to secure bead, 7ch, (1dc, 3ch, 1dc) all in next 8-ch loop, [4ch, slide a small bead up close to the hook and make 1ch to secure bead, 4ch, (1dc, 3ch, 1dc) all in next 8-ch loop] twice; rep from *, 1ss in first dc.

Fasten off.

Weave in any loose ends. Then dampen the cover, pin out and leave to dry.

Double-crochet coin purse

⊗ *This little purse is made from a basic pattern for working double crochet in the round, so you can adapt it to make other round items – a striped cushion cover for example.*

You will need
- 2 x 5g skeins of *Anchor Pearl Cotton No. 5* cotton embroidery thread in 5 colours:
  Pale lilac (shade no. 109)
  Rose (shade no. 70)
  Dusty rose (shade no. 970)
  Orange (shade no. 333)
  Light purple (shade no. 98)
- 1.50mm (US 6 steel) crochet hook
- 30 round or square beads, 4–5mm in diameter
- Zipper 15cm (6in) long
- Fabric for lining (optional)

Tension and finished size
- Approximately 21 rounds of dc forms a circle 11.5cm (4¹/₂in) in diameter using 1.50mm (US 6 steel) hook.
- Finished coin purse measures 12.5cm (5in) in diameter.

Special notes
- To keep track of where the crochet rounds start and finish, position a strand of contrasting yarn at the end of each round. To do this, before starting the next round, place the contrasting strand across the crochet fabric from front to back, close up against the loop on the hook and *above the working yarn*. Next, start to work the first double crochet of the following round,

catching the marker in position. The marker marks the start of the round and is caught under the top of the first stitch of the round.
- To change to a new colour, drop the colour you are working with when there are two loops on the hook and complete the dc with the new colour. Work over the ends of the threads to avoid having to weave them in later.

To make coin purse
The coin purse is made from two circular pieces and the colours are used at random.

FRONT
To begin, using 1.50mm (US 6 steel) hook and chosen colour, make 4ch and join with a ss in first ch to form a ring.
Round 1 (RS) 1ch, 8dc in ring. (Do not turn at end of rounds, but work with RS always facing.)
Position marker as explained in Special Note above.
Round 2 2dc in each dc. (16dc)
Round 3 *1dc in next dc, 2dc in next dc; rep from *. (24dc)
Change colours throughout as desired (see Special Note) **and at the same time** work the circle patt as foll:
Round 4 1dc in each dc.
Round 5 *1dc in next dc, 2dc in next dc; rep from *. (36dc)
Round 6 As round 4.
Round 7 *1dc in each of next 2dc, 2dc in next dc; rep from *. (48dc)
Round 8 As round 4.

Round 9 *1dc in each of next 3dc, 2dc in next dc; rep from *. (60dc)

Round 10 As round 4.

Round 11 *1dc in each of next 4dc, 2dc in next dc; rep from *. (72dc)

Round 12 As round 4.

Round 13 *1dc in each of next 5dc, 2dc in next dc; rep from *. (84dc)

Round 14 As round 4.

Cont in this way, adding 12 extra dc in every alternate round and working in random stripes until the coin purse measures 11.5cm (4½in) in diameter (about 21 rounds), ending with an increase round.

Work 1ss in next st and fasten off.

BACK

Make as for front, working random stripes or matching them to front.

To finish

Weave in loose ends and press each piece lightly on WS.

BEAD EDGING

Thread 30 beads onto the yarn so they are ready to use while crocheting. Holding the two circles with wrong sides together, work the bead edging through both layers as foll:

Insert the hook in a dc through both circles, yrh and draw yarn through, 1ch, 1dc in same dc as ch was worked, 1dc in next dc, *slide bead up close to hook and work 1ch, 1dc in each of next 3dc; rep from * until an opening 14–15cm (5½–6in) long (for zipper) remains, then work in dc around opening. Fasten off.

Backstitch zipper to opening.

Line bag with fabric if desired.

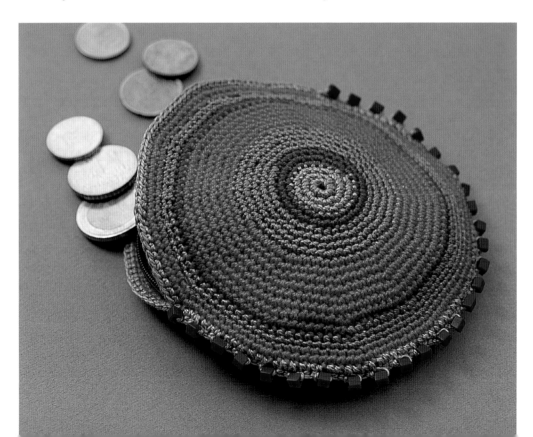

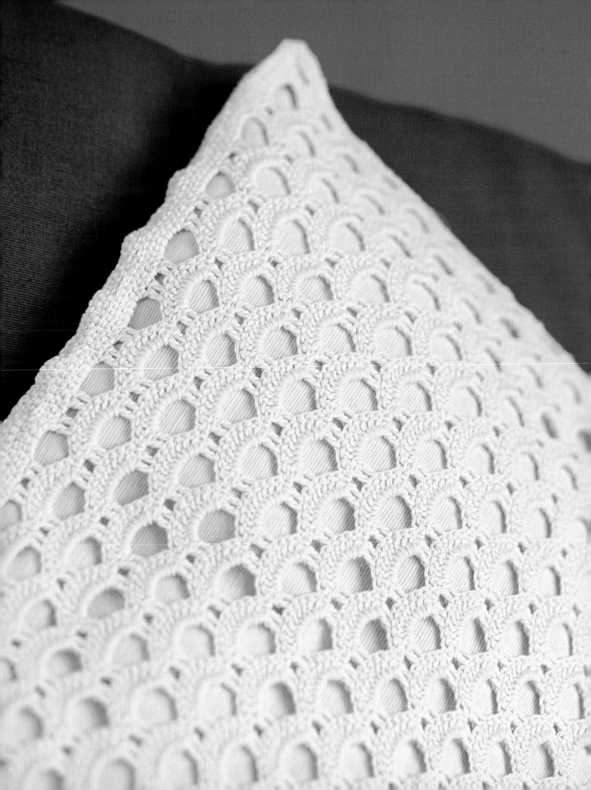

Scallop cushion

⭐ *Quick and easy to make, this cushion cover could be made in any colour you like. The lining shows through, so choose a matching one.*

You will need

- 5 x 50g balls of *Coats Lyric 8/4* lightweight cotton yarn in off-white (shade no. 5002)
- 3.00mm (US D-3) crochet hook
- Covered cushion 45cm (18in) square in desired background colour

Tension and finished size

- Each scallop repeat measures 3.5cm (1½in) wide and 2cm (¾in) deep.
- Crocheted cover measures 45cm (18in) square, not including edging.

To make cushion cover

The cushion cover is made from two identical pieces.

FRONT AND BACK (BOTH ALIKE)

To begin, make 119ch. (The first row of the pattern is worked over a multiple of 9ch, plus 2ch extra.)

Row 1 1dc in 2nd ch from hook, 1dc in each of next 2ch, *5ch, miss next 4ch, 1dc in each of next 5ch; rep from * omitting 5dc at end of last rep, 1dc in each of last 3ch. Turn.

Row 2 (RS) 1ch, 1dc in first dc, *9tr in next 5-ch loop, miss next 2dc, 1dc in next dc; rep from *. Turn.

Row 3 6ch, miss first dc and first 2tr, *1tr in each of next 2tr, 1ch, miss next tr, 1tr in each of next 2tr, 5ch, miss next 5 sts; rep from * omitting 5ch at end of last rep, 2ch, miss next 2 sts, 1dtr in last dc. Turn.

Row 4 3ch, 4tr in first 2-ch sp, *1dc in next 1-ch sp, 9tr in next 5-ch loop; rep from * to last 1-ch sp, 1dc in last 1-ch sp, 4tr in last loop, 1tr in 4th of 6ch. Turn.

Row 5 3ch, miss first tr, 1tr in each of next 2tr, *5ch, miss next 5 sts, 1tr in each of next 2tr, 1ch, miss next tr, 1tr in each of next 2tr; rep from *, ending with 5ch, miss next 5 sts, 1tr in each of next 2tr, 1tr in 3rd of 3ch. Turn.

Row 6 1ch, 1dc in first tr, *9tr in next 5-ch loop, 1dc in next 1-ch sp; rep from * to last 5-ch loop, 9tr in last 5-ch loop, miss next 2tr, 1dc in 3rd of 3ch. Turn.

Rep rows 3–6 to form patt. Cont in patt until front measures 45cm (18in) from beg, ending with a 3rd or 5th patt row. Fasten off.

EDGING

Work a dc edging around front as foll:

Round 1 With RS facing, insert hook through edge of front at any corner, yrh and draw yarn through, work 1ch, 1dc in same place as ch was worked; then working 3dc in each corner, work dc evenly around edge of front and join with a ss in first dc. (Do not turn at end of rounds, but work with RS always facing.)

Round 2 (RS) 1ch, 1dc in same place as ss, then work 1dc in each dc along sides and 3dc in each corner dc, and join with a ss in first dc. Fasten off.

To finish

Weave in any loose ends. With wrong sides facing and stitching just below edging, sew front and back together around three sides. Insert covered cushion and finish seam.

Double-crochet scarf

⭐ *Worked lengthways in double crochet, this soft, cosy cotton scarf is very easy and quick to make. It is trimmed with a self-fringe of twisted strands.*

You will need

- *Coats Lyric 8/8* medium-weight cotton yarn:
    3 x 50g balls in main colour (**MC**) – beige (shade no. 5003)
    1 x 50g ball each in 4 contrasting colours: **A** – coral (shade no. 5025); **B** – brick (shade no. 5065); **C** – purple (shade no. 5028); **D** – orange (shade no. 5037)
- 5.50mm (US I-9) and 6.00mm (US J-10) crochet hooks

Tension and finished size

- 13 stitches and 15 rows to 10cm (4in) over dc using 5.50mm (US I-9) hook.
- Scarf measures 15cm (6in) x 165cm (66in).

To make scarf

The scarf is worked from end to end instead of from side to side in order to create stripes that run lengthways.

Each row of the scarf is worked with a new strand of yarn, so that there are loose ends of yarn at each end to make a twisted fringe. To begin, using 6.00mm (US J-10) hook and MC and leaving a 25cm (10in) long loose end, make 215ch. Cut off MC, again leaving a 25cm (10in) long loose end, and fasten off by pulling the end through the last ch.

Change to 5.50mm (US I-9) hook and cont.

Row 1 Using MC again and leaving a 25cm (10in) long loose end at edge, insert hook through first ch, yrh and draw yarn through, 1ch, 1dc in first ch (same ch as hook was first inserted), 1dc in each of rem ch. Turn. (215dc)

Cut off MC, leaving a 25cm (10in) long loose end, and fasten off by pulling the end through the last dc.

Row 2 Using A and leaving a long loose end at edge as before, insert hook through first dc, yrh and draw yarn through, 1ch, 1dc in first dc (same dc as ch was worked), 1dc in each of rem dc. Turn.

Cut off A, leaving a 25cm (10in) long loose end, and fasten off as before.

Rep 2nd row 21 times more **and at the same time** leaving long loose ends at each end of every row as before, work 21-row stripe sequence as foll:

1 row B, 1 row C, 1 row B, 1 row A, 3 rows MC, 1 row D, 5 rows MC, 1 row A, 1 row B, 1 row A, 2 rows MC, 1 row D, 2 rows MC. Fasten off.

TWISTED FRINGE

Each strand of twisted fringe is made up of two loose ends of yarn. To make the twisted fringe, first knot the strands together two at a time across each end, close to the edge of the crochet. Then take one pair of knotted strands and twist each strand individually in the same direction until it starts to kink. Place the twisted strands together and twist them both in the opposite direction so they wrap around each other. Knot the end of the twisted pair 7.5cm (3in) from the edge of the crochet and trim the end. Do the same with each pair of strands.

Cotton afghan

⊕⊕ *These cotton crochet afghan squares are worked in four simple rounds. Use them for a throw, as per instructions, or a cushion cover.*

You will need

- *Coats Lyric 8/8* medium-weight cotton yarn:
  9 x 50g balls for centre colour of
  motif (**A**) – light blue (shade no. 5055)
  14 x 50g balls for middle colour of
  motif (**B**) – purple (shade no. 5028)
  20 x 50g balls for border colour of
  motif (**C**) – mid blue (shade no. 5011)
- 4.00mm (US G-6) crochet hook

Tension and finished size

- Each motif measures 12.5cm (5in) square.
- Afghan measures 125cm (50in) x 175cm (70in).

Special note

Work over the loose ends of the yarn to avoid lots of weaving in ends later.

To make afghan

The afghan is made up of 140 motifs. (You can make more motifs to alter the size, but this will alter the amount of yarn required.)

MOTIF

To begin, using A make 8ch and join with a ss in first ch to form a ring.

Round 1 (RS) 3ch, 1tr in ring, (7ch, 1ss in top of last tr, 5tr in ring) 3 times, 7ch, 1ss in top of last tr, 3tr in ring, 1ss in 3rd of first 3ch. Fasten off.

Round 2 With RS facing and using B, insert hook through first 7-ch loop made on previous round, yrh and draw yarn through (place this 'joining' st at base of 7-ch loop on right-hand side), 4ch, work [2tr, (3ch, 3tr) 3 times] all in same 7-ch loop, *miss next free tr on first round, 1ss in each of next 2tr, work [(3tr, 3ch) 3 times, 3tr] in all in next 7-ch loop; rep from *, ending with miss 1tr, 1ss in each of next 2tr, 1ss in 4th of first 4ch. Fasten off.

Round 3 With RS facing and using C, insert hook through first 3-ch loop made on previous round, yrh and draw yarn through, 1ch, 1dc in same loop, *4ch, work (1dc, 3ch, 1dc) all in next 3-ch loop, 4ch, 1dc in next 3-ch loop, 5ch, 1dc in next 3-ch loop; rep from * omitting 1dc at end of last rep, 1ss in first dc. Do not turn.

Round 4 3ch, *4tr in next 4-ch loop, 1tr in next dc, work (2tr, 2ch, 2tr) all in next 3-ch loop, 1tr in next dc, 4tr in next 4-ch loop, 1tr in next dc, 1ch, 1dc in next 5-ch sp, 1ch, 1tr in next dc; rep from * omitting 1tr at end of last rep, 1ss in 3rd of first 3ch. Fasten off. Make 139 more motifs.

To finish

Weave in any loose ends.

Using C, oversew squares together, first joining 14 rows of 10 motifs each, then joining the rows.

EDGING

With RS facing and using B, work dc evenly around edge, working 1dc in each stitch and each chain space, and working 3dc in each corner. At end of round, join with a ss to first dc. Fasten off.

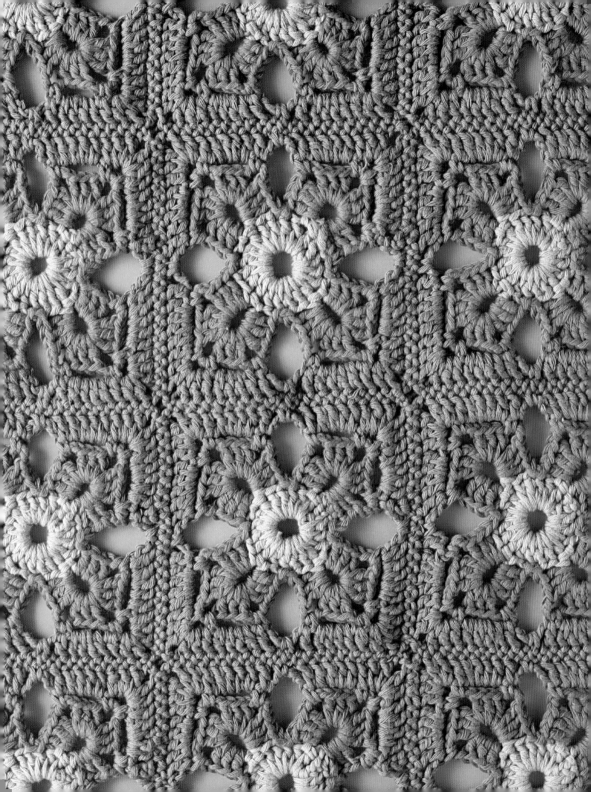

Wool afghan

✪✪ *The instructions here are for an afghan but you could make just a few squares and make a cushion cover instead. The colour scheme here is created from a 9-square repeat.*

You will need

- *Patons Diploma Gold DK* wool-mix double-knitting weight yarn:

    10 x 50g balls in main colour used for border row of each motif (**MC**) – black (shade no. 06183)

    5 x 50g balls in first contrasting colour (**A**) – light rose (shade no. 06239)

    5 x 50g balls in second contrasting colour (**B**) – mid rose (shade no. 06240)

    5 x 50g balls in third contrasting colour (**C**) – grey (shade no. 06184)

- 5.00mm (US H-8) crochet hook

Tension and finished size

- Each motif measures 9.5cm (3¾in) square.
- Afghan measures 114cm (45in) x 152cm (60in).

To make afghan

The afghan is made up of 192 motifs. (You can make more or fewer motifs to alter the size, but this will alter the amount of yarn required.)

MOTIF

To begin, using A make 6ch and join with a ss in first ch to form a ring.

Round 1 (RS) Using A, 3ch, 1tr in ring, (1ch, 2tr in ring) 3 times, 1ch, 1ss in 3rd of first 3ch. Fasten off.

Working with RS always facing, cont as foll:

Round 2 Using B, insert hook through first 1-ch sp made on previous round, yrh and draw yarn through – called *join with a ss* – , 3ch, work (1tr, 1ch, 2tr) all in same 1-ch sp, *(1ch, 2tr) twice in each of next 3 1-ch sps, 1ch, 1ss in 3rd of first 3ch. Fasten off.

Round 3 Using C, join with a ss in first 1-ch sp made on previous round, 3ch, work (1tr, 1ch, 2tr) all in same 1-ch sp, *(1ch, 2tr) twice in each of next 7 1-ch sps, 1ch, 1ss in 3rd of first 3ch. Fasten off.

Round 4 Using MC, join with a ss in first 1-ch sp made on previous round, 3ch, 2tr in same 1-ch sp (corner), *(1ch, 2tr) in each of next 3 1-ch sps, 1ch, 3tr in next 1-ch sp (corner); rep from * 3 times, omitting 3tr at end of last rep, 1ss in 3rd of first 3ch. Fasten off.

Make 191 more motifs, using a different colour for each round and always using MC for round 4, but using random colours (A, B or C) for rounds 1–3.

To finish

Weave in any loose ends.

Pin out each motif with WS face up and press following instructions on yarn label.

Arrange motifs and using MC, oversew squares together, first joining 12 rows of 16 motifs each, then joining the rows.

EDGING

With RS facing and using MC, work dc evenly around edge, working 1dc in each tr and each ch sp, and working 3dc in each of four corners of afghan. At end of round, join with a ss in first dc. Fasten off.

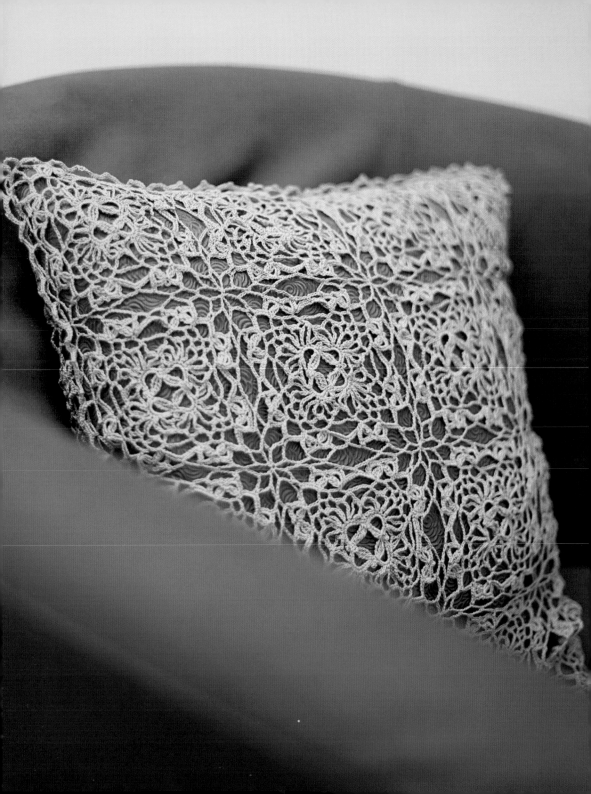

Lacy cushion

✪✪✪ *This cushion cover is a test of your crocheting skills! It has a crocheted back and front, joined together with a pretty edging to give a decorative finish. The cover is made up of lace squares which are crocheted together.*

You will need
- 6 x 20g balls of *Coats Mercer Crochet No. 20* cotton thread in chosen colour (6 motifs can be worked from one ball)
- 1.25mm (US 7 steel) crochet hook
- Covered cushion 40cm (15¾in) square in desired background colour

Tension and finished size
- Each motif measures 10cm (4in) square.
- Crocheted cover measures 40cm (15¾in) square, excluding edging.

To make cushion cover
The cushion cover is made from two identical square pieces.

FRONT AND BACK (BOTH ALIKE)
Front and back are each made up of 16 motifs.

FIRST MOTIF
To begin, make 10ch.

Round 1 (RS) *Leaving last loop of each trtr on hook work 3trtr in 10th ch from hook, yrh and draw through all 4 loops on hook (a 3-trtr cluster made), 11ch; rep from * 3 times more working 1ch instead of 11ch at end of last rep, 1ss in same ch as base of first cluster. (Do not turn at end of rounds, but work with RS always facing.)

Round 2 *12dc in next loop (this chain loop is along edge of trtr cluster), 1dc in next 1-ch sp (between cluster groups), 4ch, 1ss in last dc (a picot made); rep from *, ending with 1ss in first dc. (4 12-dc scallops)

Round 3 1ss in each of next 3dc, 1ch, 1dc in same place as last ss, *(13ch, 1dc in next dc) 5 times, 7ch, miss first 3dc of next scallop, 1dc in next dc; rep from * omitting 1dc at end of last rep, 1ss in first dc.

Round 4 1ss in each of first 5ch of first 13-ch loop, 3dc in same loop, *(5ch, 3dc in next 13-ch loop) 4 times, 1dtr in next 7-ch loop, 3dc in next 13-ch loop; rep from * omitting 3dc at end of last rep, 1ss in first dc.

Round 5 1ss in each of next 2dc and 2ch, 1dc in loop, *5ch, work [(1tr, 5ch, 1tr) in next 5-ch loop] twice, 5ch, 1dc in next 5-ch loop, 9ch, 1dc in next 5-ch loop; rep from * omitting 1dc at end of last rep, 1ss in first dc.

Round 6 1ss in each of next 2ch, 1dc in loop, *(6ch, a 3-dtr cluster in 6th ch from hook) twice (a cluster loop made), 1dc in next 5-ch loop, 9ch, 1dc in next 5-ch loop, 1 cluster loop, 1dc in next 5-ch loop, 11ch, miss next 9-ch loop, 1dc in next 5-ch loop; rep from * omitting 1dc at end of last rep, 1ss in first dc.

Round 7 *Work (4dc, 3ch, 4dc) in next loop (this chain loop is at edge of cluster), 3ch, (4dc, 3ch, 4dc) in next loop, (5dc, 5ch, 5dc) in next 9-ch loop (this forms corner scallop), (4dc, 3ch, 4dc) in next loop, 3ch, (4dc, 3ch, 4dc) in next loop, 13dc in next 11-ch loop; rep from *, ending with 1ss in first dc.

Round 8 1ss in each of next 3dc and 1ch, 1dc in 3-ch loop, *9ch, miss next 3-ch loop (loop between scallops), 1dc in next 3-ch loop, 7ch,

(1dtr, 7ch, 1dtr) in next 5-ch loop (**corner loop made**), 7ch, 1dc in next 3-ch loop, 9ch, miss next 3-ch loop, 1dc in next 3-ch loop, 4ch, miss next 10dc, 1dc in next dc (centre dc of 13-dc group), 4ch, 1dc in next 3-ch loop; rep from * omitting 1dc at end of last rep, 1ss in first dc. Fasten off.

SECOND MOTIF

Work as first motif for 7 rounds, then join to first motif on round 8. When joining motifs, hold them with wrong sides together, stitches aligned, and second motif in front. Begin the round working on the second motif only and join to first when indicated as foll:

Round 8 (joining round) 1ss in each of next 3dc and 1ch, 1dc in 3-ch loop, 9ch, miss next 3-ch loop (loop between scallops), 1dc in next 3-ch loop, 7ch, 1dtr in next 5-ch loop, 3ch, 1dc in a corresponding 7-ch corner loop on first motif, 3ch, 1dtr in same 5-ch loop on second motif, 3ch, 1dc in next 7-ch loop on first motif, 3ch, 1dc in next 3-ch loop on second motif, 4ch, 1dc in next 9-ch loop on first motif, 4ch, miss next 3-ch loop on second motif, 1dc in next 3-ch loop on second motif, 4ch, miss next 10dc on second motif and work 1dc in next dc, 4ch, 1dc in next 3-ch loop on second motif, 4ch, 1dc in next 9-ch loop on first motif, 4ch, miss next 3-ch loop on second motif and work 1dc in next 3-ch loop, 3ch, 1dc in next 7-ch loop on first motif, 3ch, 1dtr in next 5-ch loop on second motif, 3ch, 1dc in next 7-ch corner loop on first motif, 3ch, 1dtr in same 5-ch loop on second motif and complete as round 8 of first motif (from where it says 'corner loop made').

Make 4 rows of 4 motifs, joining each as second motif was joined to first. Where 4 corners meet, join third and fourth motifs to joining of previous motifs.

Dampen, pin out and leave to dry.

To finish

Place back and front with wrong sides together and join together while working edging as foll:

EDGING

Round 1 Working through both sections, attach crochet thread to second loop to right of any free corner loop, 1dc in same place as join, 9ch, 1dc in next loop, 19ch, **work (1dc, 5ch, 1dc) in next corner loop, *(9ch, 1dc in next loop) twice, 9ch, – leaving the last loop of each tr on hook and working in front section only, miss next dc, 1tr in next dc on front section and 1tr in corresponding dc on back section, yrh and draw through all 3 loops on hook (a joint tr made) – , (9ch, working through both sections work 1dc in next loop) twice, 9ch, 1dc in next join of motifs; rep from * 3 times more omitting 1dc at end of last rep; rep from ** twice more, work (1dc, 5ch, 1dc) in next corner loop, (9ch, 1dc in next loop) twice, ***9ch, working in front section only, miss next dc, 1tr in next dc, (9ch, 1dc in next loop) twice, 9ch, 1dc in next join of motifs (9ch, 1dc in next loop) twice; rep from *** twice more, 9ch, miss next dc, 1tr in next dc, 9ch, 1ss in first dc.
Round 2 Work (5dc, 3ch, 5dc) in each of next 2 loops, *work (3dc, 3ch, 3dc) in next 5-ch loop, work (5dc, 3ch, 5dc) in each 9-ch loop along side; rep from * 3 times more, ending with 1ss in first dc. Fasten off.
Dampen and press edging.
Insert covered cushion and sew together opening.

Each motif of the Lacy Cushion is joined to its neighbour in the 8th round. This close-up shows the crochet stitches that join four motifs where they meet at a corner to create a star shape.

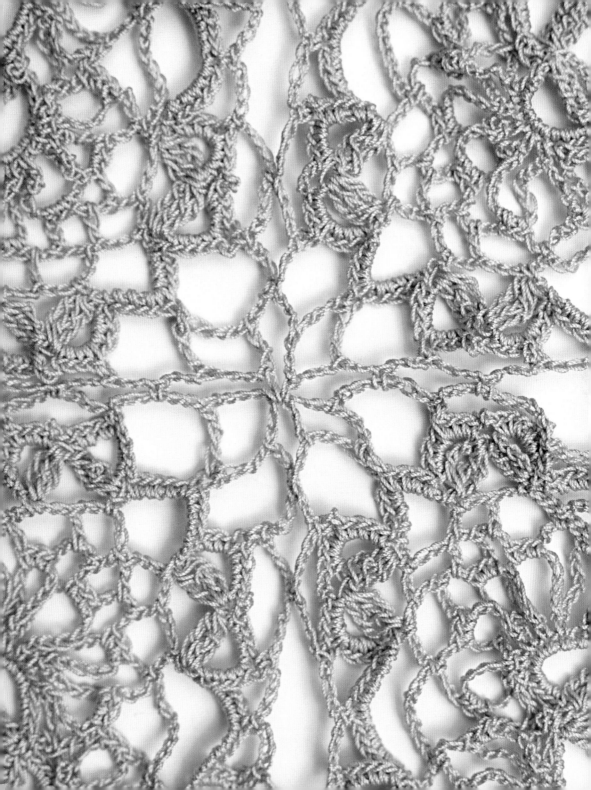

Hand towel edging

✪✪ *This simple edging adorns a cotton piqué guest towel, but you could, just as easily, use it for a pillowcase, if you prefer. The edging is made separately then stitched in place, and you can adjust the length to suit that of your own towel. Fine white crochet cotton thread has been used to make the scallops, although a heavier weight yarn or a coloured one would work equally well.*

You will need
- 1 x 50g ball of *Coats Aida No. 5* crochet cotton thread in chosen colour
- 1.50mm (US 6 steel) crochet hook
- Hand towel of your choice

Tension and finished size
- The edging measures 4cm (1½in) deep (once blocked) and each pattern repeat measures 4cm (1½in) across. Finished length is adjustable.

To make edging
Before beginning, calculate how many scallops are needed to fit your towel.

To begin, make 14ch for each pattern repeat needed except the last, and make 13ch more for the last pattern repeat. (The first row is worked over a multiple of 14ch, plus 13ch extra.) The edging shown is 32cm (12in) long and the foundation chain needed for this length is 111ch.

Row 1 (RS) 1dc in 2nd ch from hook, 1dc in each of rem ch. Turn. (110dc)

Row 2 1ch, 1dc in each of first 4dc, 5ch, miss next 4dc, 1dc in next dc, *(3ch, miss next 2dc, 1dc in next dc) 3 times, 5ch, miss next 4dc, 1dc in next dc; rep from * to last 3dc, 1dc in each of last 3dc. Turn.

Row 3 1ch, 1dc in first dc, *(5tr, 5ch, 5tr) all in first 5-ch loop (a scallop made), (1dc in next 3-ch loop, 3ch) twice, 1dc in next 3-ch loop; rep from * to last 5-ch loop, 1 scallop in last 5-ch loop, miss next 3dc, 1dc in last dc. Turn.

Row 4 5ch, (1dc, 3ch, 1dc) all in 5-ch loop of first scallop, *2ch, 1dtr in next 3-ch loop, 11ch, 1dtr in next 3-ch loop, 2ch, (1dc, 3ch, 1dc) all in 5-ch loop of next scallop; rep from *, ending with 1trtr in last dc. Turn.

Row 5 1ch, (1dc, 3ch, 1dc) all in first 3-ch loop, *15tr in next 11-ch loop, (1dc, 3ch, 1dc) all in next 3-ch loop; rep from * to end. Fasten off.

Dampen edging, pin out and leave to dry. Sew edging to one end of hand towel.

Made in only five rows, this edging is quite easy to make. If you're looking for an alternative edging, turn to pages 26 and 27 and take your pick. You'll find some even simpler edgings there.

Filet pillow

✪✪ *Four blocks of filet crochet form the centrepiece of a gingham cushion, but you could also create an entire cushion from similar squares, which are joined together. Then add the filet edging shown on page 71 as a border if you wish.*

You will need
- 1 x 20g ball *Coats Mercer Crochet No. 20* cotton thread in chosen colour
- 1.25mm (US 7 steel) crochet hook
- Covered cushion of desired size

Tension and finished size
- 20 sps and 20 rows to 10cm (4in) using 1.25mm (US 7 steel) hook.
- Each motif measures 9.5cm (3¾in) square.
- Four joined motifs measure 19cm (7½in) square.

Special note
Filet crochet is made up of spaces (sps) and blocks (blks) of treble stitches. Start the pattern following the written instructions to see how the blocks and spaces are made and then continue working from the chart alone (turn to page 25 for the chart).

To make filet for pillow
The filet for the pillow is made from 4 motifs.
MOTIF
To begin, make 60ch.
Row 1 1tr in 4th ch from hook, 1tr in each of next 2ch, (2ch, miss next 2ch, 1tr in next ch) 17 times (17 sps made), 1tr in each of next 3ch. Turn.

Row 2 5ch, miss first 3tr, 1tr in next tr (sp made at beg of row), (2tr in next 2-ch sp, 1tr in next tr) 17 times (17 blks made over 17 sps), 2ch, miss next 2tr, 1tr in next ch (sp made over blk at end of row). Turn.
Row 3 5ch, miss first tr, 1tr in next tr (sp made over sp at beg of row), 1tr in each of next 3tr (1 blk made over 1 blk), (2ch, miss next 2tr, 1tr in next tr) 15 times (15 sps made over 15 blks), 1 blk, 2ch, miss next 2ch, 1tr in next ch (sp made over sp at end of row). Turn.
Continue to follow diagram from 4th to 18th row (see page 25).
19th row 3ch, 2tr in first sp, 1tr in next tr (blk made at beg of row), 17 sps, 2tr in next sp, 1tr in 3rd of 5ch (blk made at end of row). Fasten off.
Make 3 motifs more in same way.

To finish
Weave in loose ends.
Oversew four motifs neatly together, making two rows of two motifs.
EDGING
Work a row of dc evenly around edge, working 3dc in each corner and ending with a ss in first dc. Fasten off.
Dampen crochet, pin out and leave to dry.
Stitch to centre of cushion cover.

Pillowcase edgings

★★ *These little lace edgings are ideal for a pillowcase. One has simple picots, the other is an uncomplicated filet design. Adjust the length and colours to suit your own bed linens, and if you wish, use a finer thread (such as gauge 20), with a finer hook (1.25mm/US 7 steel).*

You will need
- 1 x 50g ball of *Coats Aida No. 10* crochet cotton or 1 x 50g ball *Coats Eldorado* crochet cotton in chosen colour
- 1.50mm (US 6 steel) crochet hook
- Pillowcase of your choice

Tension and finished size
- **FILET EDGING**
  The filet edging measures 3.5cm (1¹/₂in) deep, and there are 15 rows to 10cm (4in) using 1.50mm (US 6 steel) hook.
  Can be worked to required length.
- **PICOT EDGING**
  The picot edging measures 3.5cm (1¹/₂in) deep and each scallop repeat measures 2.5cm (1in) across using 1.50mm (US 6 steel) hook.
  Length is adjustable.

To make filet edging
To begin, make 20ch.
Row 1 1tr in 8th ch from hook, *2ch, miss next 2ch, 1tr in next ch; rep from *. Turn.
Row 2 5ch, miss first tr, 1tr in next tr, (2tr in next 2-ch sp, 1tr in next tr) 3 times, 2ch, miss next 2ch, 1tr in next ch. Turn.
Row 3 5ch, miss first tr, 1tr in each of next 4tr, 2ch, miss next 2tr, 1tr in next ch of next 4tr, 2ch, miss next 2ch, 1tr in next ch. Turn.
Row 4 5ch, miss first tr, 1tr in each of next 4tr, 2tr in next 2-ch sp, 1tr in each of next 4tr, 2ch, miss next 2ch, 1tr in next ch. Turn.
Row 5 5ch, miss first tr, 1tr in next tr, (2ch, miss next 2tr, 1tr in next tr) 3 times, 2ch, miss next 2ch, 1tr in next ch. Turn.
Rep rows 2–5 until edging is required length, ending with a 4th patt row.
Fasten off.

To make picot edging
Before beginning, calculate how many picoted scallops are needed to fit your pillowcase.
Make 10ch for each scallop needed, then make 3ch extra for edge stitches. (The first row is worked over a multiple of 10ch, plus 3ch extra.) The edging shown is 40cm (16in) long and the foundation chain needed for this length is 163ch.
Row 1 (RS) 1dc in 2nd ch from hook, 1dc in each of rem ch. Turn.
Row 2 1ch, 1dc in each of first 2dc, 2ch, miss next 2dc, 1 dc in next dc, *9ch, miss next 2dc, 1dc in next dc, 2ch, miss next 2dc, 1dc in each of next 2dc, 2ch, miss next 2dc, 1dc in next dc; rep from * to last 7dc, 9ch, miss next 2dc, 1dc in next dc, 2ch, miss next 2dc, 1dc in each of last 2dc. Turn.
Row 3 1ch, 1dc in each of first 2dc, work [(3tr, 3ch) 3 times, 3tr] all in next 9-ch loop, miss next dc, *1dc in each of next 2dc, work [(3tr, 3ch) 3 times, 3tr] all in next 9-ch loop, miss next dc; rep from *, ending with 1dc in each of last 2dc. Turn.

Row 4 4ch, 1dc in first 3-ch loop, 4ch, work (1dc, 3ch, 1dc) all in next 3-ch loop, *4ch, 1dc in each of next 2 3-ch loops, 4ch, work (1dc, 3ch, 1dc) all in next 3-ch loop; rep from *, ending with 4ch, 1dc in next 3-ch loop, 4ch, 1ss in last dc. Turn.
5th row *(5dc in next 4-ch loop) twice, work [(1dc, 3ch) 3 times, 1dc] all in next 3-ch loop; rep from *, ending with work (5dc in next 4-ch loop) twice.
Fasten off.

To finish edgings
Dampen edging, pin out and leave to dry. Sew edge of crochet edging to edge of pillowcase with matching thread.

Christmas decorations

✪✪✪ *These little motifs make great Christmas decorations (suitably stiffened and hung on pretty ribbons), but you could alternatively hang them on cupboard doors or at the window. Adding beads or using metallicized yarns gives them a festive touch. Once made, they will need to be stiffened with a sugar solution or with starch.*

You will need
- 1 x 20g ball of *Coats Mercer Crochet No. 20* cotton thread in white (one ball will make all four decorations)
- 1.25mm (US 7 steel) crochet hook
- Beads to decorate – 8 for eight-pointed star, 6 for six-pointed star, 4 for diamond
- Narrow ribbon for hanging

Finished sizes
- Six-pointed star measures 9cm (3½in) in diameter.
- Eight-pointed star measures 7.5cm (3in) in diameter.
- Diamond measures 7.5cm (3in) square.
- Snowflake measures 9.5cm (3¾in) in diameter.

To make eight-pointed star
Before beginning, thread 8 beads onto the crochet cotton.
To begin, make 16ch and join with a ss in first ch to form a ring.
Round 1 (RS) 32dc in ring, 1ss in first dc. (Do not turn as end of rounds, but work with RS always facing.)
Round 2 1ch, 1dc in same place as ss, *15ch, 1dc in each of next 2dc; rep from * omitting 1dc at end of last rep, 1ss in first dc. (16 15-ch loops)
Round 3 1ss in each of first 6ch of first 15-ch loop, 1ch, 3dc in same loop, *2ch, work (1dc, 5ch, 1dtr, 5ch, 1dc) all in next loop, 2ch, 3dc in next loop; rep from * omitting 3dc at end of last rep, 1ss in first dc of first 3-dc group.
Round 4 1ss in next dc, 6ch, *1dc in next 2-ch sp, work (1dc, 1htr, 5tr) all in next 5-ch loop, 1tr in next dtr, work (5tr, 1htr, 1dc) all in next 5-ch loop, 1dc in next 2-ch sp, 3ch, miss next dc, 1tr in next dc (centre dc of 3-dc group), 3ch; rep from * omitting 1tr and 3ch at end of last rep, 1ss in 3rd of first 6ch.
Round 5 (bead round) 1ch, 1dc in same place as ss, *7ch, work (1dc, 1ch, slide bead up close to work, 2ch – first of these ch secures bead in place – , 1dc) all in tr at centre of next point, 7ch, 1dc in tr between next 2 3-ch sps; rep from * omitting 1dc at end of last rep, 1ss in first dc.
Fasten off.

To make six-pointed star
Before beginning, thread 6 beads onto the crochet cotton.
To begin, make 14ch and join with a ss in first ch to form a ring.
Round 1 (RS) 24dc in ring, 1ss in first dc. (Do not turn as end of rounds, but work with RS always facing.)

Shown from left to right are the eight-pointed star, the six-pointed star and the diamond motif.

Round 2 4ch, 1dtr in same place as ss, *3ch, (2dtr in next dc) twice; rep from *, ending with 3ch, 2dtr in next dc, 1ss in 4th of first 4ch. (12 3-ch sps)

Round 3 1ss in next dtr, 1ss in first ch of next 3-ch sp, 1dc in same 3-ch sp, *4ch, 1dc in next 3-ch sp; rep from *, ending with 4ch, 1ss in first dc.

Round 4 *Work (1dc, 1htr, 3tr, 1htr, 1dc) all in next 4-ch loop; rep from *, ending with 1ss in first dc. (12 scallops)

Round 5 1ss in each of next 2 sts, 1dc in next st (centre tr of scallop), *5ch, – leaving the last loop of each dtr on hook, work 1dtr in next tr, miss next 4 sts, 1dtr in next st, yrh and draw through all 3 loops on hook (a joint dtr made) – , 5ch, 1dc in next st (centre tr of scallop), 8ch, miss next 6 sts, 1dc in next st (centre tr of scallop); rep from * omitting 1dc at end of last rep, 1ss in first dc.

Round 6 1ss in first ch of next 5-ch loop, 3ch, 7tr in same 5-ch loop, *3ch, 8tr in next 5-ch loop, work (1dc, 3ch, 1dc) all in next 8-ch loop, 8tr in next 5-ch loop; rep from * omitting 8tr at end of last rep; 1ss in 3rd of first 3ch.

Round 7 (bead round) 1ss in each of next 7tr, 1ss in first ch of next 3-ch loop, 8ch, slide bead up close to hook, 2ch – first of these ch secures bead in place – , 1ss in 4th ch from hook, 2ch, 1dtr in same 3-ch loop, *7ch, work (1dc, 3ch, 1dc) all in next 3-ch loop, 7ch, work (1dtr, 4ch, slide bead up close to hook, 2ch, 1ss in 4th ch from hook, 2ch, 1dtr) all in same 3-ch loop (V-st made); rep from * omitting V-st at end of last rep, 1ss in 4th of first ch made. Fasten off.

For a glittery effect, make the star decorations with a metallic thread, such as *Anchor Orion*, and add silver beads.

To make diamond

Before beginning, thread 4 beads onto the crochet cotton.
To begin, make 2ch.

Round 1 (RS) 6dc in 2nd ch from hook, 1ss in first dc. (Do not turn as end of rounds, but work with RS always facing.)

Round 2 3ch (to count as first tr), 1tr in same place as ss, 2tr in each of rem 5dc, 1ss in 3rd of first 3ch. (12 sts)

Round 3 1ch, 1dc in same place as ss, *(11ch, 1dc in next tr) twice, 17ch, 1dc in next tr; rep from * omitting 1dc at end of last rep, 1ss in first dc. (4 17-ch corner loops and 8 11-ch loops)

Round 4 1ss in each of first 4ch of first 11-ch loop, 1ch, 2dc in same loop, *2ch, 2dc in next 11-ch loop, 6ch, 3dc in next 17-ch loop, 6ch, 2dc in next 11-ch loop; rep from * omitting 2dc at end of last rep, 1ss in first dc.

Round 5 1ss in next dc, 1ss in first ch of first 2-ch sp, 1dc in same sp, *3ch, work (1dc, 1htr, 7tr, 1htr, 1dc) all in next 6-ch loop, 3ch, miss next dc, 1dc in next dc (centre dc of 3-dc group), 3ch, work (1dc, 1htr, 7tr, 1htr, 1dc) all in next 6-ch loop, 3ch, 1dc in next 2-ch sp; rep from * omitting 1dc at end of last rep, 1ss in first dc.

Round 6 1ss in first ch of first 3-ch loop, 1dc in same loop, *7ch, work (1dtr, 8ch, 1dc) all in next 3-ch loop, work (1dc, 8ch, 1dtr) all in next 3-ch loop, 7ch, 1dc in next 3-ch loop, 3ch, 1dc in next 3-ch loop; rep from * omitting 1dc at end of last rep, 1ss in first dc.

Round 7 *Work [(1dc, 1htr, 7tr, 1htr, 1dc) all in next loop] 4 times, work (1dc, 7ch, 1dc) all in next loop; rep from *, ending with 1ss in first dc.

Round 8 1ss in each of next 5 sts, 1ch, 1dc in same place as last ss, *7ch, 1dc in centre tr of next scallop, 7ch, slide bead up close to hook, 2ch – first of these ch secures bead in place – , 1ss in 4th ch from hook, 6ch, 1dc in centre tr of next scallop, 7ch, 1dc in centre tr of next scallop, 3ch, 1dc in next 7-ch loop, 3ch, 1dc in centre tr of next scallop; rep from * omitting last dc at end of last rep, 1ss in first dc. Fasten off.

To make snowflake

To begin, make 20ch and join with a ss in first ch to form a ring.

Round 1 (RS) 4ch (to count as first dtr), 39dtr in ring, 1ss in 4th of first 4ch. (Do not turn as end of rounds, but work with RS always facing.)

Round 2 1ch, 1dc in same place as ss, 1dc in each of next 3dtr, *work [(1dc, 5ch) 3 times, 1dc] all in front loop only of next dtr (a triple picot made), 1dc in each of next 4dtr; rep from * omitting 4dc at end of last rep, 1ss in first dc. (8 triple picots)

Round 3 1ch, 1dc in same place as ss, *4ch, 1dtr in each of next 2dc, 4ch, 1dc in next dc, working behind next triple picot work 1 triple picot in back loop of next dtr on first round, 1dc in first dc of next 4-dc group; rep from * omitting 1dc at end of last rep, 1ss in first dc.

Round 4 1ss in each of next 4ch and in next dtr, 4ch, 2dtr in same place as last ss, *3ch, 3dtr in next dtr, 5ch, 3dtr in next dtr; rep from * omitting 3dtr at end of last rep, 1ss in 4th of first 4ch.

Round 5 1ch, 1dc in same place as ss, 1dc in each of next 2dtr, *3dc in next 3-ch sp, 1dc in each of next 3dtr, 5dc in next 5-ch sp, 1dc in each of next 3dtr; rep from * omitting 3dc at end of last rep, 1ss in first dc.

Round 6 1ch, 1dc in same place as ss, 1dc in each of next 3dc, *work 1 triple picot in front loop only of next dc, 1dc in each of next 4dc, 7ch, miss next 5dc, 1dc in each of next 4dc; rep from * omitting 4dc at end of last rep, 1ss in first dc.

Round 7 1ch, 1dc in same place as ss, 1dc in each of next 3dc, *work 1 triple picot in back loop of next dc on round 5, 1dc in each of next 4dc, 5ch, 1dc in next 7-ch loop, 5ch, 1dc in each of next 4dc; rep from * omitting 4dc at end of last rep, 1ss in first dc.

Round 8 1ch, 1dc in same place as ss, *9ch, 1ss in 4th ch from hook, 6ch, miss (3dc, a triple picot, and 3dc) and work 1dc in next dc, 7ch, – leaving the last loop of each dtr on hook work 1dtr in each of next 2 5-ch loops, yrh and draw through all 3 loops on hook (a joint dtr made) – , 7ch, 1dc in next dc; rep from * omitting 1dc at end of last rep, 1ss in first dc.

Fasten off.

To finish all decorations

Weave in loose ends.

To stiffen the crochet decorations, starch them. Alternatively, mix 3 tablespoons caster sugar with 1/2 cup water, bring to the boil while stirring, then leave to cool. Dip the crochet in this sugar-water bath and shake out excess water. Pin out carefully and leave to dry.

Use lengths of ribbon to hang the decorations. Loop the centre of the ribbon through the edge of the decoration and tie the ends together.

For an interesting alternative hanging cord, crochet a beaded one. Simply thread small beads onto the crochet cotton, then work a length of chain, sliding a bead into place on every 4th or 5th chain.

The snowflake motif is adorned with delicate little three-dimensional flowers that are made as the rounds are worked, of loops of chain stitches.

Yarn/thread information

Buying yarn

For the best results, use the yarn/thread specified for a particular pattern (see next page for addresses). If you cannot obtain the specified yarn, use the yarn specifications below to help obtain a similar substitute. Always calculate how much yarn you need by metrage/yardage rather than weight.

Yarn specifications and care

The following yarns/threads were used for the projects in this book. A recommended crochet or knitting tension is given where available. Although the care instructions are listed below, always double-check the yarn label in case care instructions have altered since the publication of this book.

ANCHOR MAGIC

- Description: Medium-weight cotton yarn.
- Fibre content: 100 per cent mercerized cotton.
- Ball size: 50g ball (approximately 70m/76yd).
- Care: Machine-washable up to 40°C on wool cycle with minimum machine action; may be pressed with hot iron; may be dry cleaned in solvents indicated on label; do not bleach; do not put in dryer.

ANCHOR ORION

- Description: Metallic crochet thread.
- Fibre content: 62 per cent metallicized polyester and 38 per cent nylon.
- Ball size: 10g ball (approximately 133m/145yd).

- Care: Machine-washable up to 30°C; press with cool iron only; may be dry cleaned in solvents indicated on label; do not bleach; do not put in dryer.

ANCHOR PEARL COTTON (NO. 5)

- Description: Shiny, twisted embroidery thread.
- Fibre content: 100 per cent cotton.
- Skein size: 5g skein (approximately 22m/24yd).
- Care: Machine-washable up to 95°C; may be pressed with hot iron; may be dry cleaned in solvents indicated on label.

COATS AIDA NO. 10 AND NO. 5

- Description: Cotton crochet thread.
- Fibre content: 100 per cent mercerized cotton.
- Ball size: 50g ball (No. 10 approximately 280m/306yd; No. 5 approximately 200m/219yd).
- Care: Machine-washable up to 95°C; press with warm iron only; may be dry cleaned in solvents indicated on label; do not bleach; do not put in dryer.
- Recommended crochet hook sizes: 1.25mm–1.50mm (US sizes 7–6 steel).

COATS ELDORADO

- Description: Cotton crochet thread.
- Fibre content: 100 per cent mercerized cotton.
- Ball size: 50g ball (approximately 265m/290yd).
- Care: Machine-washable up to 95°C; may

be pressed with hot iron; may be dry cleaned in solvents indicated on label; do not bleach.
- Recommended crochet hook size: 1.50mm (US size 6 steel).
- Recommended crochet tension: 35 stitches and 17 rows to 10cm (4in) measured over treble crochet using 1.50mm (US size 6 steel) hook.

COATS LYRIC **8/4**
- Description: Lightweight cotton yarn.
- Fibre content: 100 per cent cotton.
- Ball size: 50g ball (approximately 150m/164yd).
- Care: Machine-washable up to 95°C; may be pressed with hot iron; may be dry cleaned in solvents indicated on label; do not bleach; do not put in dryer.
- Recommended crochet hook size: 3.00mm (US size D-3).
- Recommended crochet tension: 24 stitches and 10 rows to 10cm (4in) measured over treble crochet using 3.00mm (US size D-3) hook.

COATS LYRIC **8/8**
- Description: Medium-weight cotton yarn.
- Fibre content: 100 per cent cotton.
- Ball size: 50g ball (approximately 70m/76yd).
- Care: Machine-washable up to 95°C; may be pressed with hot iron; may be dry cleaned in solvents indicated on label; do not bleach; do not put in dryer.
- Recommended crochet hook size: 4.00mm (US size G-6).
- Recommended crochet tension: 18 stitches and 8 rows to 10cm (4in) measured over treble crochet using 4.00mm (US size G-6) hook.

COATS MERCER CROCHET NO. 20
- Description: Cotton crochet thread.
- Fibre content: 100 per cent mercerized cotton.
- Ball size: 20g ball (approximately 145m/158yd).
- Care: Washable up to 60°C; press with cool iron only; do not dry clean; do not bleach.
- Recommended crochet hook size: 1.25mm (US size 7 steel).

PATONS DIPLOMA GOLD DK
- Description: A wool-mix, double-knitting weight (medium-weight) yarn.
- Fibre content: 55 per cent wool, 25 per cent acrylic and 20 per cent nylon.
- Ball size: 50g (approximately 120m/131yd).
- Care: Machine-washable in warm water up to 40°C on wool cycle with minimum machine action; may be dried in dryer at 60°C; press with cool iron under dry cloth (never wet press); may be dry cleaned in solvents indicated on label; do not bleach.
- Recommended knitting tension: 22 stitches and 30 rows to 10cm (4in) measured over stocking stitch using 4mm (US size 6) needles.

Suppliers and acknowledgments

For information on stockists and suppliers of yarns and equipment mentioned in this book please contact Coats Crafts UK, as follows:

Coats Crafts UK
Lingfield Point
McMullen Road
Darlington
Co. Durham
DL1 1YJ
UK
Tel +44 (0) 1325 394394
www.coatscrafts.co.uk

The publishers would like to thank the following for their help with this book: John Heseltine for the photography (except for pages 50, 52 and 72 by Steven Wooster); Anne Wilson for the design; Kate Simunek for the artwork; and Tracey Whittington at Coats Crafts UK for supplying yarns, threads and equipment.